ROAD SIGNS

FOR CATHOLIC TEENS

Our Sunday Visitor

www.osv.com
Our Sunday Visitor Publishing Division
Our Sunday Visitor, Inc.
Huntington, Indiana 46750

Nihil Obstat:
Msgr. Michael Heintz, Ph.D.
Censor Librorum

Imprimatur:
✠ Kevin C. Rhoades
Bishop of Fort Wayne-South Bend
November 19, 2018

The *Nihil Obstat* and *Imprimatur* are declarations that a work is free from doctrinal and moral error. It is not implied that those who have granted the *Nihil Obstat* and *Imprimatur* agree with the contents, opinions, or statements expressed.

Our Sunday Visitor Publishing Division
Our Sunday Visitor, Inc.
200 Noll Plaza
Huntington, IN 46750
1-800-348-2440

ISBN: 978-1-68192-296-6 (Inventory No. T1972)
eISBN: 978-1-68192-297-3
LCCN: 2019931647

Cover design: Chelsea Alt
Cover art: Shutterstock
Interior design: Chelsea Alt
Interior art: Shutterstock.com; Public Domain; BoalMuseum.com; Wikimedia Commons via Abraham Sobkowski, OFM, Sswonk, Kenneth C. Zirkel, Roseohioresident; KansasTravel.org, AuriesvilleShrine.com; FranciscanCaring.org; Flickr via Terry Robinson; Nancy Dendy Geerts

PRINTED IN THE UNITED STATES OF AMERICA

DEDICATED TO THE HOLY FAMILY

CONTENTS

BEGINNING THE JOURNEY

Jennessa Terraccino

Go in peace. The journey on which you go is under the eye of the Lord.

JUDGES 18:6

The silver key glimmered in the light and jingled against the others, as my dad dangled the keychain. With my newly minted driver's license in my pocket, I saw those car keys as a true treasure. When I grabbed them from my father's fingers, I was filled with a mix of emotions — fear, a sense of responsibility, excitement, and a spirit of adventure. You know what that feeling is like. Getting your hands on the wheel for the very first time means you are the one in control. While you're in the driver's seat, the choices you make and the turns you take are yours alone.

Where is the first place you want to drive solo? That initial trip might be to the school parking lot, but surely you have bigger travel plans for your parents' old mini-van. Your driving experience would get rather boring if you never left the driveway, and rather dull if you never ventured out of your hometown. You have roads to explore, places to go, a world to see; and of course, along the way, potholes to avoid and traffic jams to encounter. The monumental occasion of getting your license is just one more outward sign that you are growing up.

Did you know that, on average, American drivers over the age of eighteen spend nearly eighteen hours and thirty-one minutes a week in their car?[1] That means drivers spend over five days behind the wheel each month! Pretty soon, if you aren't already, you will be spending a lot of time behind the wheel. Most of us don't think much about driving; it's just the process of getting from point A to point B. But what if your car could be more than just a means of transportation? What if — with the right vision — you could see the road differently?

Whether we realize it or not, all of us are more than just drivers. We're pilgrims on the road of life. A pilgrim is someone who is on a journey with a specific, very important destination in mind. For us, as Christian pilgrims, the road trip of our lives is taking us to a sacred place. Determination, focus, and fidelity are crucial if we are to arrive at our planned destination: heaven.

Driving means you aren't a kid anymore. "When I was a child, I spoke like a child, I thought like a child, I reasoned like a child; when I became a man, I gave up childish ways" (1 Cor 13:11). As a licensed teen, your parents won't be driving you everywhere all the time, and that might even include Mass. This moment, when you are starting to embrace adulthood, is the moment to take over the keys of your spiritual life too. While you may have to wait to own a car, you can own your faith now.

When we're on a road trip, it's absolutely crucial to follow the road signs. The road signs we obey while driving show us where to go and what to avoid, and help us navigate around other drivers so we don't harm ourselves or anyone else in the course of our trip. I've noticed that the more I pay attention, the more those same road signs point me to deeper, spiritual truths. The rules and guidelines we need to follow to safely reach our destination really apply to our whole lives.

With that in mind, it is time to navigate the open roads and take God with you. He can speak through anything, even road signs! Follow the road signs and let them point you to God. On the trip, remember that the Church is here to provide you fuel, strength, and direction. Buckle up, hit the gas, and let's go.

CROSSROAD
ACT OF FAITH

Chelsea Zimmerman

*If any man would come after me, let him deny himself and
take up his cross and follow me.*

MATTHEW 16:24

While you are on the road, you aren't always in motion. When you see a Crossroad sign, you know you will likely have to stop your vehicle for a few seconds. Once at the intersection, you, as the driver, have to look around and make some quick decisions. Are there any other cars in the intersection that have the right-of-way? Do you need to continue straight through, turn right, or turn left to continue toward your destination? Perhaps every day, you come to a particular crossroad in your route, and every day you go the same way. Yet the choice always remains. You could always choose to go in a whole new direction, a decision that would change the course of your journey.

On the road of life, you will encounter many crossroads, and they won't always be physical. More often, they will be little choices: what outfit to wear, what to eat for dinner, what movie to watch, what sport to play, or whom to sit next to in class. At times, though, you will need to tackle big choices that may alter your life's course: when to get your first car, where to go to college, what field to pursue, whether you should move out of state, whether you should go on that date, or whether you will go to Mass this Sunday. Will you turn right, turn left, or keep on along the same path?

I faced my first major crossroad in life after failing my first driver's test. Looking back, I should have taken that as a sign that I wasn't quite ready. I could have considered my parents' advice and spent more time studying the traffic laws and practicing driving with an adult; but at sixteen, I believed I was invincible. I had places to go, people to see, and parents to flee. Lacking patience and prudence, I went to a neighboring DMV to take the test a second time. I just barely passed, but freedom sang. I thought, "What's the worst that could happen?"

Beep. Beep. Beep. Beep. Beep.

The dull, constant sound in my hospital room wasn't the sound of freedom. In less than a year as a licensed driver, not only did I flip and total two cars (mine and my boyfriend's), but the last of those accidents damaged my spinal cord so badly that I became permanently paralyzed from the chest down. Though my accident did not happen at a physical crossroad, my driving mistakes brought me to an emotional crossroad. On the one hand, I could focus on the negative, feel sorry for myself, and give up on life; or I could see the many possibilities and accept the new challenge I was facing. By the grace of God, and with a lot of help from family, friends, and an amazing team of doctors, nurses, and physical therapists, I chose the latter.

Soon I found myself at another crossroad. Though I had worked hard to get out of rehab and back to my "regular" life, a lot had changed. For a variety of reasons, it wasn't very easy to go out with friends. I soon found myself with a lot of unexpected and unfamiliar alone time. There, in a "still small voice," God spoke to my heart (1 Kgs 19:11–13). I spent much of that time reflecting on the accident, my injury, and what it all meant. It occurred to

PIT STOP

MACKINAC BRIDGE
St. Ignace, Michigan

Driving to Michigan's spectacularly beautiful Upper Peninsula involves crossing this five-mile-long suspension bridge. You'll see Lake Huron out of one window and Lake Michigan from the other.

me how very easily I could have died in that accident. In fact, for a while there, the doctors had not been sure I was going to make it. In the year before my accident, several teenagers had died on the roads out where I lived. Two of them were from my school and younger than me. Suddenly, I was all too aware of the imminence of death. I was forced to ask myself: Was I prepared?

My honest answer? No.

In his book *Preparation for Death*, Saint Alphonsus de Liguori writes: "My brother, if you wish to live well, spend the remaining days of life with death before your eyes."[2] A priest from our day, Monsignor Charles Pope, suggests a similar tool to avoid temptation: "Meditate frequently on death, especially at night before going to bed."[3] It sounds morbid, but awareness of the certainty of death helps put life in perspective. Not only does it prompt us to cherish our own life and the lives of our loved ones, but it also helps us to remember for what we are really living. As pilgrims, "we have no lasting city, but we seek the city which is to come" (Heb 13:14). It's time to get serious about getting to the Eternal City.

After my accident, as my soul sat idling at the biggest crossroad of my life, I realized that I had lost sight of where I was headed. It wasn't so much that I had consciously pushed aside prayer or developing my spiritual life, but my many earthly pursuits — school, job, friends, boyfriend, and more — were the main focus in my life.

ROADSIDE DISTRACTIONS

Unclaimed Baggage Center

Scottsboro, Alabama

Shopping trip! The UBC is the size of a city block, and in its sprawling interior you can roam through the bargain-priced contents of very lost luggage.

Sure, I went to Mass every Sunday with my family, but I had abandoned any real, personal relationship with Jesus Christ; as a result my faith was no longer evident in the way I lived my life. Holiness, I had implicitly decided, was something that I would worry about later, when I was older and settled down and closer to the final years of my life. It never occurred to me that the end of my life could come so soon. But I had been given a second chance. I understood that I had to get serious — now!

Right now, as a teenager, you are at a crossroad of faith. The choice is yours to make: you can continue along the same road, passively going through the motions of faith; you could turn away from Christ completely; or you could turn toward him and allow that choice to penetrate every corner of your life. Being Catholic is not merely a social identity. It's not a question of what lowercase "c" church you belong to or attend. It is a question of conviction. What do I believe? Do I accept the truth Jesus Christ reveals? For whom am I living ? Am I ready to commit my entire self — intellect and will, mind and heart — to God? Is my faith evident in the way I live my life? Do I give my faith fervent expression liturgically and sacramentally; through prayer, acts of charity, a concern for justice, and respect for God's creation? Is my faith fruitful? Take a moment and really dwell on these questions.

On this road that we travel you will receive an endless amount of invitations to "follow." They will come in the form of people, virtual profiles, movements to join, relativism, other religions, or temptations to a wide variety of sins. Yet in the end, none of these solicitations matter compared to the immeasurable invitation of Jesus. He invites us to a more abundant life, a life with meaning and purpose and direction.

Sometimes it is easy to follow, never taking true ownership of our faith in Christ and just going through the motions. When it comes to faith and your entrance into heaven, however, you can't ride the coattails of someone else. It doesn't matter that five hundred people saw the resurrected Jesus (cf. 1 Cor 15:6), or that your friend Joe believes in Jesus. Those are great testaments of Christ, but you have to believe personally, and make that belief real in your life.

Perhaps what is most challenging about faith is that this is not a choice you make only once. You will face the crossroad of faith again and again. In Baptism we arc washed clean of all sin, and we become part of God's chosen (*Catechism of the Catholic Church* 1263–1270), but our pilgrimage doesn't end there. In Confirmation we are united more fully to Christ (CCC 1303), but the journey doesn't end there either. With each new day you will be confronted with the reality of your free will. In life, as in driving, you will come to many crossroads. Often, you may have to make a decision that requires an act of faith. Sometimes the choice will be easy, but sometimes what's right is not what's popular, and a decision could put you at odds with your friends or even your family.

Have you responded to Jesus' invitation lately? He beckons and says, "Follow me" (Mt 4:19). Do you know how much Jesus loves you? He suffered, died, and rose from the dead for each and every sinner — for you. He offers each of us the free gift of grace. As a sinner in need of saving, what is your personal response to Jesus, the Savior? Just like you've taken charge of the driver's seat, now is the time to own your faith, taking it from your head to your heart.

HOLY ROAD TRIP

CHRIST OF THE OZARKS
Eureka Springs, Arkansas

This seven-story-tall white statue of Christ towers over the trees and stands as the landmark for a huge Passion Play put on every year.

Meet Jesus there. He is the Savior, *your* Savior, but he is also your friend (cf. Jn 15:15).

A true and personal experience with Christ leads to authentic faith. "It is no longer because of your words that we believe, for we have heard for ourselves, and we know that this is indeed the Savior of the world" (Jn 4:42). Jesus is the only path of salvation (see "One Way: Truth and Life"). As you approach the crossroad, his arms are outstretched to you. It is time to embrace him. Jesus' invitation is to "bear much fruit, and so prove to be my disciples" (Jn 15:8). Respond to his invitation with an act of faith (in your own words, or use the prayer below) in this moment.

> *O my God, I firmly believe that you are one God in three Divine Persons — Father, Son, and Holy Spirit; I believe that your divine Son became man, and died for our sins, and that he will come to judge the living and the dead. I believe these and all the truths the holy Catholic Church teaches because you have revealed them, who can neither deceive nor be deceived.*

Renew your desire for discipleship daily.

The Crossroad sign can also remind us of the cross of Christ. "[R]eal discipleship," Archbishop Charles J. Chaput writes in his book *Render Unto Caesar*, "always has a cost."[4] It "demands more than reading about the Catholic faith or admiring the life of Jesus."[5] Jesus didn't ask that we simply agree with him, but that we follow him, and "we cannot follow Christ without sharing in his cross."[6]

When encountering the cross, our initial response may be to reject it. We pull our hands away from hot stoves, wince at the sight of a needle, cry in times of sorrow, and run from difficulties. Who is anxious to carry someone else's 200-pound cross, drenched in blood and sweat? What does it mean to take up your cross? In taking up the cross, we die to self, selfishness, self-centeredness, and self-indulgence. When we meet the cross, we meet Jesus.

When you see a Crossroad sign, may it remind you of the true cross you have the chance to move toward in every act of faith. The road won't always be easy, but we do not drive alone: Christ is with us. Jesus declares that "in the world you have tribulation; but be of good cheer, I have overcome the world (Jn 16:33)." At the crossroad of life, turn east toward the Son of man (cf. Mt 24:27), and keep on driving until you get to the holy city, the New Jerusalem (cf. Rv 21:2).

QUESTIONS FOR REFLECTION

1. At this crossroad in your life, what big choices are you facing right now?
2. What is a crossroad of faith? Do you feel that you are engaged in your faith, and truly living for Christ? How can you seek to have a more personal relationship with Jesus, and take ownership of your faith?
3. What does it mean to take up your cross? What does your current cross look like? How can we unite our sufferings with the cross of Christ?

ONE WAY
TRUTH AND LIFE

Mattias Caro

I am the way, and the truth, and the life.

JOHN 14:6

When you are learning to drive, you are given a driver's manual. After algebra and chemistry textbooks, this manual is quite unintimidating; it's even thinner than the directions to assemble a piece of furniture. As you know by now, the booklet is filled with information like useful roadway tips, turn-signal instructions, and explanations of signs like Stop, Go, Yield, and the simple black and white rectangular One Way. At first these signs seem simple — just word, shape, and color combinations; but put them together on the side of the road, and these signs begin to guide you, the driver, through complex roadways.

Those basic One Way signs, for instance, are super useful. Many cities are laid out in a grid pattern — if you look at the city from above, the streets seemingly intersect like the lattice top of mom's apple pie crust. Ever wonder why those downtown streets don't have two-way traffic? The biggest reason is congestion. When streets are so close together, splitting up the flow of the traffic helps a large number of cars move around smoothly. City planners figured this out during horse-and-buggy times; it works now, and it'll probably still work when we have flying cars.

To say streets are One Way is well and good. No one seems to have a problem with obeying this rule of the road, because drivers don't want to get run over by an eighteen-wheeler! But also, One Way signs reveal a certain design, a smart design, which also takes into consideration the road pattern of the city as a whole. We all know that the design did not just magically appear, but conforms to the plan of the designer, and at some basic level makes sense. Even if you can't see the whole plan with a bird's eye, you trust that following this rule of the road will get you to where you need to go.

We generally don't have a hard time understanding that a One Way sign exists for a reason and that our lives are easier if we follow it. Yet, somehow we don't all feel this way when we apply the same principle to beliefs. Christ says, "I am the way, and the truth, and the life" (Jn 14:6). The Lord makes a very clear statement: we can only get to heaven through him. Jesus is the Savior of the world. Saint Peter, when filled with the Holy Spirit, declares "there is salvation in no one else, for there is no other name under heaven given among men by which we must be saved" (Acts 4:12). In other words, we already possess the map to heaven.

Just like we face threats on the road every time we drive, we also face threats to our faith. One of those perils is relativism, which claims the road to heaven isn't One Way. Instead, this false philosophy declares that there are many equally valid paths to salvation. Today, people believe that Jesus is just one option out of many. Relativism suggests that what's true for one person may not be true for another. But is truth based on personal opinions or preferences? Can you imagine if, while driving, what may be a one-way road to you could simultaneously be a two-way road for someone else? Would you trust a driving instructor who said, "When I see a One Way sign, I like to follow it, but if

PIT STOP

CHRISTOPHER COLUMBUS CHAPEL
Boalsburg, Pennsylvania

In 1909, Theodore Boal and his wife, Mathilde de Lagarde, a descendant of Christopher Columbus, imported the explorer's chapel and its furnishings from Spain to their Pennsylvania estate.

you aren't really feeling it, you can go any direction you like. Drive however you want. I don't want to impose my beliefs on you"? If you followed those directions, you'd probably get into your first accident! This mentality doesn't work on the road, and it causes chaos in life too. Truth is truth; there is no "my" truth and "your" truth. It cannot differ from person to person.

Personal preferences can change, such as which drive-thru to go grab dinner from, or what color and make of car you'd like to drive. These choices in our life express our uniqueness, personality, and mood. Such choices cannot really be measured. It is impossible to determine if a taco or burger is objectively more delicious. What you eat, or the color of your car, has no effect on your salvation. These are simply expressions, not truth.

But moral truths that determine right or wrong, and religious beliefs, cannot be based on our mood or temperament. On the surface, relativism sounds polite and nice, and a great way of avoiding argument, but it is full of faulty logic. In fact, relativism negates itself. In declaring that there is no universal truth, one actually states a truth: that there is no universal truth.

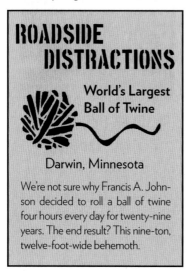

ROADSIDE DISTRACTIONS

World's Largest Ball of Twine

Darwin, Minnesota

We're not sure why Francis A. Johnson decided to roll a ball of twine four hours every day for twenty-nine years. The end result? This nine-ton, twelve-foot-wide behemoth.

Underlying every field of study from chemistry to ethics is a basic rule called the "principle of noncontradiction." That's a fancy name for the fact that two contradictory statements cannot be simultaneously true. For example, I cannot say that $2 + 2 = 4$ and also $2 + 2 = 5$. Believing those two statements at the same time would be a contradiction! Relativism says that the only truth is that there is no truth — a contradictory and impossible state of things.

Pope Benedict XVI called relativism a dictatorship.[7] He was thinking of one very sad reality: dictators tell you what to do; and in telling you what to do, they completely remove your freedom. Dictators care nothing for your individuality, who you are, or where you might be going. They only want you to go where they say you must go.

How can relativism be a dictator if the relativist says, "Believe whatever you want"?

If we believe whatever we want, can we still love Our Lord? If we love Jesus as Truth, we are committed to the reality that flows from that relationship: that Christ is not just our way, truth, and life, but as he himself said, he is the way, the truth, and the life. You can either accept Christ as the only way, or reject him. There is no in-between. You are either driving the right way down the one-way road, or you are at risk of ending up in a nasty accident.

On one level, it's important to follow the One Way street sign because if you don't, as I said, you'll probably be staring down an eighteen-wheeler. But on another, more fundamental level, we follow the One Way street signs because we want to get somewhere! If you were in Chicago (which has a nice grid system, by the way) trying to reach New York, you'd have to travel east. All directions were not created equal. You can't simply decide that you would prefer to go north to get to New York. No matter how many northbound streets you take, you would never arrive in NYC. We know that driving according to the rules will get us where we need to go. Truth isn't a matter of opinions.

As the bumper sticker declares, can't we all just "coexist"? Unfortunately, because we are talking about a dictator, relativism will not be content leaving our relationship with Christ alone. Fullness of faith is found in the Catholic Church. Just ask any of the two thousand years' (and counting!) worth of apostles, disciples, Church Fathers, and saints. It is only faith in Christ "that creates unity and is fulfilled in love."[8]

Jesus didn't die on the cross to allow humanity to coexist, but to save us from sin, and he knew it was only through him that our salvation could be accomplished. The burnt offerings of the past just didn't cut it; nor do the false philosophies of today. Similarly, morality isn't just about following arbitrary rules or self-prescribed preferences. It is about getting somewhere: heaven! More precisely, it is about choosing to be how God created us to be, in his image and likeness. When we break the rules of morality — lying, stealing, lusting, cheating — we are not just breaking the One Way sign. We are really acting contrarily to how God made us, like a bird trying to act like a fish. Relativism tells us, "If it feels good, do it." But God, the Second Person of the Trinity, became one of us. In doing so he said to us, "Look at me, be my friend, love me, and then, only then, will you understand and be able to be the person I have created you to be."

As you discover the person God created you to be, you wouldn't want someone to contradict your self-knowledge. Let's say you have brown hair, love to play soccer, play the guitar, and just acquired your driver's license. If a peer began a conversation with you and told you that you played basketball, not soccer, because they did not like that sport, you'd seek to correct them. You might be a bit annoyed if they said you had red hair and not brown. Perhaps they were also convinced that you played the trumpet, not the guitar, and that you were not old enough for a driver's license. You would begin to wonder if they were even speaking about you. Despite your revealing yourself and your outward appearance, what if this peer refused to acknowledge the truth about you? I think you would be baffled and even bothered. Jesus revealed himself to us in truth. He doesn't need us rewriting his image or truth. You cannot simply make God whatever you want him to be, or choose what is right and wrong. As we have seen, Jesus is "the way, and the truth, and the life," and "God is love" (1 Jn 4:8).

True love — as we all know in the deep relationships of family and friendship we have and cultivate — does not happen overnight. Nor is it merely a feeling. If it were a feeling, then it could disappear whenever we wanted it to (we would make love a slave to our feelings — sounds like relativism!). Love is a commitment, of our hearts and minds, of our actions and of our energies, to someone. Love happens over a long period of time, and it survives many, many ups and downs.

Christ calls us to true love with him. This call isn't just for us, but also for our friends, whether or not they share the gift of our Catholic faith. When at the end of time God judges our actions, he will not primarily look to see whether or not we were a good person (although that is part of the equation). He will look us in the eye and, in an instant, we will know whether or not we love him! The dictator of relativism wants us to have no room in our hearts for that love because that love is absolute, concrete, unchanging, and true. In this life, the only way we know to truly grow in that love is to grow closer in our relationship with Christ,[9] especially through prayer, through the sacraments, and through the Church!

HOLY ROAD TRIP

AVE MARIA GROTTO
Cullman, Alabama

Here you'll find miniature reproductions of pilgrimage sites and landmarks from around the world, built by a Benedictine monk out of found objects and a lot of love.

We follow a One Way sign because we know we want to get somewhere, and we'd like to get there on a safe, direct route. Thus, when we say Christ is the way, we might ask quickly, where are we going? We are going to him, to heaven! He provided us with the map to get to him, when he gave us his holy Church and holy Word. When we teach others that Christ is the One Way (and when we fight this dictatorship of relativism), we do not do so because we want to show we are right and others are wrong. Honestly, nothing could be more boring than proving you are right and others are wrong! No, we talk about Christ as the One Way because we want others to share in the love we have for him. Which is really caring about someone: giving them the truth, or letting them drive the wrong direction both literally and morally?

If you find yourself struggling with this truth, may I invite you to deepen your life of prayer? Love requires spending time with your loved one. Spend time with Jesus in prayer, especially with him in the Blessed Sacrament (see "Rest Area: Prayer").

Also, share this gift of faith with others. Respect for others is not the same as indifference. If someone is driving the wrong direction on a one-way street, we shouldn't shrug our shoulders about it and say "Whatever, if that's what is right for them." We'd seek to help them for their sake and the sake of the other drivers. Our love of Christ should be contagious. Our Lord beautifully revealed to us that God is our Father. Even when you are with friends who are not Catholic, invite them to pray the Our Father with you. How beautiful to place the words that were once on Christ's lips on the lips of others. Sometimes it is only through a quiet invitation to experience something as simple and as beautiful as this prayer that a heart will suddenly open up to Christ's love. That is the One Way we are all seeking, and that we should all share.

Questions for Reflection

1. What is relativism? Why is it a contradiction? Why can't you believe in both relativism and Christianity?
2. What do you think Jesus meant when he said, "I am the way, and the truth, and the life" (Jn 14:6)?
3. What is the difference between an opinion and an objective moral truth?
4. If a peer contradicted your self-knowledge by describing you incorrectly, despite your revealing yourself, how would this make you feel?

ROAD NARROWS
HEAVEN

Jonna Schuster

For the gate is narrow and the way is hard, that leads to life, and those who find it are few.

MATTHEW 7:14

A few years ago, I drove a jeepload of high school girls to our annual fall retreat. Expectations were high, joy had settled over the car, and we happily chatted and sang along to soundtracks for the three-hour trip. Eventually, we arrived at the home I had rented us for the weekend. This was our first time visiting this retreat site, so I was unaware that upon entering the property the driveway suddenly narrowed to a single-lane gravel road that wound through the woods for almost two miles before reaching the house. When I say single lane, I mean the lane was *exactly* the width of my jeep, with no shoulder on either side, and lined on both sides by trees the entire way. Also, it was pitch-black outside.

Suddenly, our carefree drive turned into the most intense game of "don't lose the side mirrors on my car" of all time. For those two miles, every muscle in my body was tense as I peered over my steering wheel and strained to see as much as I possibly could in my high beams. My speed slowed to a crawl, and I was on high alert, all too aware that I had precious lives in my car to protect besides my own. When the warm lights of the home came into view, and I could park the car and finally let my muscles relax, I was awash with relief.

In speaking about heaven, Jesus said, "Enter by the narrow gate, for the gate is wide and the way is easy that leads to destruction, and those who enter by it are many. For the gate is narrow and the way is hard, that leads to life, and those who find it are few" (Mt 7:14). My driving experience has given me a new appreciation for Jesus' exhortation. When driving, we encounter a Road Narrows sign only while we are on a comparatively wider road which is about to narrow. (I would have appreciated this warning when I pulled onto that retreat property!) The image that Jesus paints for us implies that, at some point, we need to make the choice to leave our initial path and enter by the narrow gate if we want to experience the richness of life that he promises. Interestingly, Jesus doesn't state that the wide road is necessarily filled with bad things; only that it's dangerous, because its end point is destruction.

Let's be honest: we all want to be happy. The wide road of our culture presents many options for us to choose from in pursuing happiness. Self-improvement is one of the most popular categories you'll find on the market, and there is no shortage of strategies, products, and lifestyles that can help us live more fulfilling lives. Although a few of these things are just plain bad news, many (if not most) contain some degree of goodness and truth in them that we can appreciate. But there's a reason Jesus said that, at some point, the journey to true life — life to the full (cf. Jn 10:10) — must take us through the narrow gate and onto the narrow road. As good as many resources or self-improvement strategies may be, they can only get us so far. They might be able to offer a measure of joy, peace, healing, or fulfillment, but there is a limit to what they can give. By inviting us to enter the narrow gate, Jesus is offering us an alternative that has lasting effects, brings

PIT STOP

PLYMOUTH ROCK
Plymouth, Massachusetts

Yep, that Plymouth Rock, from American history class. Take a road trip to Massachusetts and you can see the granite boulder marking where the English Pilgrims landed for the first time.

total fulfillment, and is drastically less burdensome than other regimens that rely solely on human effort. Jesus is not just another self-improvement strategy. He is the gate to a relationship with the Father, the gate to heaven — to the presence of God, the fruit of which is healing, freedom, wholeness, and ultimate fulfillment, starting right now and extending beyond our death into eternity. Jesus makes fullness of life possible, not by giving us rules and strategies to follow, but by opening up a connection to the Father that no other way or shortcut can access. That relationship is not something you can earn or achieve; it is something you receive by choosing to follow him.

This may seem strange to you, but I daydream about heaven literally every day. While I'd like to say it's a strategic discipline to help me keep my eye on the finish line, in actuality I've been doing it since I was a child, simply because I am fascinated by it and helplessly drawn to it.

When I do my best to imagine heaven — the best of the best of everything — I often go back to the scene that is painted for us at the beginning of the Bible in the book of Genesis: the Garden of Eden, before sin entered the picture (cf. Gn 2:8–25). Adam and Eve enjoyed a lush landscape covered in flora and fauna, deep human companionship, and complete freedom. They had purpose and fulfillment in a place entirely saturated with the presence of God, not to mention face-to-face encounters with God himself. It's also worth noting what is *not* present in this garden: pain, sickness, torment, disease, fear, shame, struggle, death … every affliction of the soul and body is completely absent. No poverty, no hunger, no brokenness, no lack, no division, no anger, no fighting, no hatred, no confusion. There is perfect order, perfect unity, and perfect relationship among God, mankind, and creation.

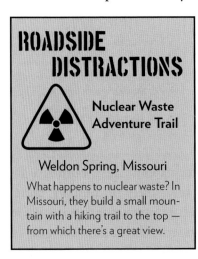

ROADSIDE DISTRACTIONS

Nuclear Waste Adventure Trail

Weldon Spring, Missouri

What happens to nuclear waste? In Missouri, they build a small mountain with a hiking trail to the top — from which there's a great view.

As Catholic Christians, it's important to remember that this was God's original design for man — for us. From the moment that Adam fell and broke that perfect harmony, God enacted the rescue mission of all rescue missions: the quest to restore us to our original design, free from sin, sickness, torment, and captivity; fully connected in relationship to God, one another, and creation; operating in the fullness of our identity, potential, and calling; and living as powerful world-changers and love-bringers, just like our heavenly Father.

How do we access heaven? Through Jesus. When he died, Jesus tore the veil that separated heaven and earth. Back in biblical times, inside the Temple, a veil separated everyone from the Holy of Holies (the inner chamber where they believed the presence of God dwelled). The Holy of Holies was so sacred that the only person allowed to enter was the high priest, once a year. He had to do so wearing a rope tied around him, the end of which remained on the outside of the veil, so that just in case he died while within, his body could be retrieved without anyone else having to enter the Holy of Holies. Intense, right? But when Jesus died, the temple veil was torn in two (cf. Mt 27:51), signifying that the separation was destroyed, giving each of us full access to God. This new access brought a radical shift in the way God wanted to relate to us: as sons and daughters to the most kind, wonderful Father who wants to be present to us at all times with no limit. Full access to his presence. And guess what? Heaven is described in Scripture most simply as God's presence (cf. Rv 21:2–3, 23). In fact, the *Catechism of the Catholic Church* describes heaven with the simple phrase: "the 'place' of God" (CCC 326). That may sound underwhelming, but remember what life was like for Adam in Eden: constantly abiding with God; enjoying complete freedom, wholeness, and fulfillment; everything as it should be. It's a package deal. In the presence of God, that is the default status. No degree of brokenness or imperfection can stand in his presence, just as darkness has no choice but to yield when a light turns on. In the midst of the difficulty and pain we experience in our current world, doesn't that sound fabulously appealing?

Once we enter the narrow gate and begin to travel that road to heaven, though, there is a warning. The road is narrow, and as I learned from navigating to that retreat, narrow roads can be intense. Why might Jesus want to warn us about this? Things that are incompatible with God's values and design cannot stand in his presence. That includes sin, brokenness, and any bad habits or coping mechanisms that we develop to deal with the broken things in our lives. When we start down the narrow road of following Jesus toward our eternal destination, we'll receive glimpses of heaven along the way … but pain and difficulty will often arise as well. Taking this road requires vulnerability. It means letting Jesus into our brokenness and shame and the darkest corners of our hearts, so as to heal, restore, and recalibrate us to his standards. These standards are good and life-giving and far preferable to survival mode, but our brokenness and coping mechanisms can be comfortable. It's often easier to numb and distract ourselves, or to work at our issues by our own human strength, than to let go and let Jesus in to do the work that's needed. That vulnerability is scary. It can hurt to lose old friendships, even if they were causing damage in our lives. It can be difficult to navigate life without certain habits we've learned, even if they were bad or harmful toward others. I was fortunate that as I drove that narrow retreat road my jeep was able to (just barely) fit in the lane. Had I been driving a different vehicle, arriving at my final destination might have required losing my side mirrors along the way, or scraping off a layer of paint. Sometimes the circumstances and conditions of our lives require sacrifices along the way in order to get to our heavenly destination, and some of us may need to make greater sacrifices than others. But the pain of those sacrifices is temporary and worth it.

When Jesus restored what was lost in the Fall, he set

a new standard for a wildly radical, never-before-seen lifestyle that even Jesus had to use parables to describe. He called it "the kingdom of heaven" (Mt 4:17). Here's the outrageous thing that Jesus taught about heaven: It's not just some unknown distant future or place that we all hope to arrive at after death. It is a kingdom — God's kingdom — the principles of which he taught his followers to live by here and now, from the way we respond to conflict (cf. Mt 5:43–47) to the way we handle sickness and oppression (cf. Mt 10:1), to the way we steward resources (cf. Mk 6:34–44), to the way we view impossibilities (cf. Mt 14:24–29). All these things have a completely different approach along the narrow road than on the wider path, so Jesus spent the final three years of his life teaching and training his followers how to recalibrate to the values and principles of his heavenly kingdom and labor with him to bring about the restoration of the earth (cf. Mt 9:35–10:1; Mk 16:15–18). For this reason, heaven can be described as an "already-but-not-yet" reality. God's kingdom is coming and is here in some measure (cf. Mt 10:7), but it has not yet been realized in its fullness. It is a process that has already begun on earth and will be completed when Jesus returns at the end of time to judge the world and set

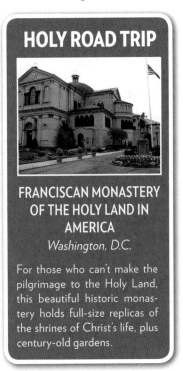

HOLY ROAD TRIP

FRANCISCAN MONASTERY OF THE HOLY LAND IN AMERICA
Washington, D.C.

For those who can't make the pilgrimage to the Holy Land, this beautiful historic monastery holds full-size replicas of the shrines of Christ's life, plus century-old gardens.

everything right. In the meantime, we are instructed to pray for the kingdom to increase: "Your kingdom come ... on earth as it is in heaven" (Mt 6:10), and we are commissioned to do the things of the kingdom on earth. So we await that final day, but even before our earthly lives end, we can experience very real aspects of heaven right here and now. The lifestyle of the narrow road not only serves to increase our hunger and affection for the kingdom and the God for which we were made, but also will sanctify us—preparing our hearts, minds, bodies, and souls for the eternal home we hope to enjoy with Our Lord in heaven. But it all starts with connection to Jesus.

There are no shortcuts in life, and, as Jesus tells us through this road imagery, there are no shortcuts to heaven. Any wider roads can only offer a counterfeit of true wholeness or fulfillment — they won't last, and they'll eventually leave us bored and dissatisfied (at best) because they can get us only so far. They may offer momentary peace or a temporary solution to problems, but those results are rarely sustainable, and if we continue on these wide paths, they will also cause us eventual destruction. They will either mask the brokenness, or they'll demand that we carry the unbearable pressure to perfect ourselves by our own efforts. Either way, our brokenness will eventually destroy us if we don't bring it before the Savior, because the real solution requires the supernatural power, forgiveness, and restoration that only he can offer.

So how do we drive this narrow road to heaven? Start by entering the narrow gate. If you haven't done so yet, make the decision to ground yourself in Christ (the act of faith in "Crossroads: Act of Faith" is the perfect way to do that). From there, read up on the Gospels and the lifestyle Jesus laid out for us to follow. Imitate him, and embrace the new reality he established for us, through prayer, frequenting the sacraments, and stepping out in bold faith like the Apostles. But above all, draw close to God in friendship, anchoring yourself in the presence of our heavenly Father (cf. Mt 7:22–23). As with my driving experience, it's always important to stay attentive to the things that surround us, but the way through any difficult journey is to keep our eyes fixed on the road, on Jesus. He may illuminate the way only a few steps at a time, but he is trustworthy and faithful and will guide us to our final destination. He paid the ultimate price for us to get there, which means he wants us in heaven even more than we do! In spite of any hardship you encounter on that narrow road, the way is far more thrilling and wonderful than any alternative route, and the freedom and joy made accessible to us is real and well worth the price. Dorothy Day once said, "All the way to heaven is heaven, for He said, 'I am the Way,'"[10] so as heaven unfolds around you on this journey, don't forget to enjoy the ride!

QUESTIONS FOR REFLECTION

1. What do you imagine heaven to be like? What will not be present in heaven?
2. Why do you think the road to heaven is narrow? What may be required of us to travel it?
3. How can we be a part of the kingdom of Heaven while on earth? More specifically, what principles can we live out every day?

SLIPPERY WHEN WET
THE NEAR OCCASION OF SIN

Ben Fleser

Abstain from every form of evil.

1 THESSALONIANS 5:22

Most of us have a routine. We are creatures of habit: We wake up at the same time, on the same side of the bed. We may eat the same type of cereal every day. We use the same brand of toothpaste. We drive the same familiar route to school filled with the usual turns and traffic lights, and wave to the same neighbor every morning who walks his dog at, you guessed it, the same time. Despite the predictability of our daily drive to school or work, the way we encounter the road may be different on any given day because of our mood, bad weather, or distractions like an incoming text message. One day when I was driving to high school with a friend, things got way too slick on the pavement I had traveled hundreds of times. In torrential rain, my friend lost control of the car, and we did a 360-degree turn in the middle of the road. We were safe, but it was a close call — I can still feel my heart pounding!

How easy it is to begin to swerve on the road of our

lives, particularly if we're trying to drive the narrow road to heaven. The journey can feel long and difficult, and is often filled with potholes, ditches, roadblocks, rain, ice, and other slippery situations! Those dangers are the result of that divisive three-letter word: sin. What exactly is this spiritual slippery patch? The *Catechism of the Catholic Church* tells us, "Sin is an offense against God. ... Like the first sin, it is disobedience, a revolt against God through the will to become 'like gods,' knowing and determining good and evil" (CCC 1850; see also Genesis 3). So, sin is separation from God, a wedge of pride we put between ourselves and God's redeeming love. Sin, then, is not merely about breaking a rule or adhering to a code of "right" and "wrong." It is about breaking a relationship with God, our loving Father.

Indeed, we are all sinners; every pope, priest, religious, and layperson (that's you). "If we say we have no sin, we deceive ourselves, and the truth is not in us" (1 Jn 1:8). Therefore, as sinners, our hope remains Jesus. He took on our very flesh, yet conquered sin and death through his passion, death, and resurrection. We must never lose sight of him. In a culture of hypersensitivity, sin has become something socially taboo, something uncomfortable to discuss. Pope Benedict XVI once boldly stated, "The ways of the Lord are not easy, but we were not created for an easy life, but for great things, for goodness."[11] Life isn't about comfort; it's about greatness! We are called to be saints one day in heaven where true greatness will finally be had. In order to achieve this everlasting greatness and find that peace we long for, we have to confront our weaknesses and occasions of sin.

Over the years, you have probably learned the difference between venial and mortal sins. But it is just as important to avoid the near occasions of sin: persons, places, or things that may easily lead you to sin (cf. 1 Cor 15:33). Just like the road sign Slippery When Wet warns a driver of a potentially hazardous situation, Jesus warns us about the need to prevent sin entering our lives: "And if your eye causes you to sin, pluck it out; it is better for you to enter the kingdom

NATIONAL SEPTEMBER 11 MEMORIAL & MUSEUM
New York City, New York

September 11 changed our country and the world. Take a detour to remember and pray at this beautiful memorial and museum located at the original site of the towers.

of God with one eye than with two eyes to be thrown into hell" (Mk 9:47). While Jesus is not actually promoting self-mutilation, he uses powerful words to convey an important message: if you want to get to heaven, remove the objects and places in your life that might cause you to slip; that is, to sin.

The near occasion of sin involves placing yourself in a situation where, even though you have not yet committed a sin, you may be enticed or led to do so. We all know those situations or have encountered them before. It could be attending a party with immoral activities, spending too much alone time with your boyfriend/girlfriend, placing too much focus or attention on gossip, or idly surfing the Internet late at night. When we say "yes" to such occasions, we put ourselves in risky situations where we could slip into sin, which could lead us to an eternal dead end (see "Dead End: Hell")! As Saint

Mark said, "Watch and pray that you may not enter into temptation; the spirit indeed is willing, but the flesh is weak" (Mk 14:38). Since Adam and Eve sinned in the Garden, humanity suffers from an inclination to sin and evil called *concupiscence*. To conquer this inclination, we have to remove ourselves from vulnerable situations where we will give in to temptation.

We have to learn to identify those situations, posting our own Slippery When Wet signs. We all have our own struggles and things we are working through, so it's up to us to reflect daily on the areas of our life that may need some work. It's also good to reflect on where we are succeeding, so we can recognize the growth and progress we've made and not fall into despair. This is also known as making an examination of conscience, which, if we make it a daily practice, is a valuable tool.

The examination of conscience helps us to reflect and to center ourselves upon God and see ourselves in the light of his presence. How did we use our time and talents to glorify him? Where were we lacking? Upon confronting our sins, we can begin to make improvements and prepare for the next time a temptation toward our recurring sins might pop up.

Our Catholic faith is not merely a book of rules that eliminates all the things we find enjoyable. The Church does not function like a traffic cop waiting for you to do something wrong in order to give you a big ol' ticket. Instead, the Church is like a tender mother who takes the keys out of her teen's hands during a bad rainstorm and says, "I think you ought to stay in tonight." Our faith is about maintaining a relationship with a person. When we seek Christ, God's laws begin to feel less burdensome, and even become desirable. "The truth will make you free" (Jn 8:32).

When I was a sophomore in college, I went to visit an old high school friend. This was a friend who had gotten into the party lifestyle while we were in high school. We were sitting outside his apartment, catching up, when suddenly he broke down in tears and started telling me about his life post–high school. He had gotten involved in hard drugs, was involved in a physically and verbally abusive relationship with his girlfriend, was entwined in sexual relationships with multiple partners, and even had threats made against his life. He looked exhausted, miserable, and unfulfilled. All the things that our culture said were supposed to bring happiness and fulfillment came up short and left him empty and depressed.

I remembered in high school feeling like I was missing out on something because my friends were going to a lot of parties while I hung back. I felt isolated sometimes, like I wasn't embracing all life had to offer. Popular culture and the media might lead us to believe that if we aren't following a particular extravagant lifestyle, we are not really living! We are missing out on all the greatness life has to offer. Unfortunately, the lifestyle they promote can be laced with selfish actions: the exploitation and objectification of the human person through pornography; drug and/or alcohol abuse; sabotaging someone's reputation through lies and spiteful gossiping; or violence and excessive aggression, to name a few. After talking with my friend, I saw how sin had taken hold of his life and cast him into a downward spiral. He had lost control of his vehicle and swerved off the road. This opened my eyes wide to the reality of hurt caused by sin. The Devil, whose deception introduced sin into the world, waits for us to let down our guard. Therefore, "Be sober, be watchful. Your adversary the devil prowls around like a roaring lion, seeking some one to devour. Resist him, firm in your faith" (1 Pt 5:8–9).

Scripture is filled with stories of human failings (cf. 2 Sm 11:2–27) like my friend's, but that is never the end of the story. We should not be discouraged by our shortcomings and weakness, because redemption is close at hand. We need Jesus.

There is more joy in heaven over one sinner who repents than over ninety-nine righteous persons (cf. Luke 15:4–7)! What love! What mercy! The words of Jesus should fill us with great hope as Our Lord emphasizes the great desire to show mercy and forgiveness toward a truly repentant heart. Jesus rejoices over those who humble themselves, admit their faults, and return to the resting place of Our Lord's Sacred Heart. "I have not come to call the righteous, but sinners to repentance" (Lk 5:32).

ROADSIDE DISTRACTIONS

Carhenge

Alliance, Nebraska

Precisely what it sounds like — an accurate replica of the original Stonehenge, made of 39 automobiles, because #art. (There's a webcam if you can't make the road trip.)

So with all this talk about sin and human frailty, what's the solution?

The Church offers us many tools to help us identify and prepare for the times when our road gets slick. Among these, frequent reception of the Holy Eucharist at Mass and invoking the prayers of Mary and the saints are among the most important. Saint John Bosco had a dream where a ship carrying the pope and all the representatives of the Church was being attacked on all sides. Then two pillars shot up from the water, one with the Holy Eucharist on top and the other with the Virgin Mary. The ship anchored itself between the two pillars and was saved.[12] The Eucharist, the Body and Blood of Our Lord, keeps us in frequent communion with him and nourishes us for the journey onward. Our Lady, the Virgin Mary, is our great spiritual mother and intercessor who leads us to the heart of Christ and guards our purity. Although these spiritual gifts are essential, we can take some personal steps to confront sin and avoid it in the future:

1. Be Accountable: What fun is a road trip without at least one passenger? As Christians, we need the community of the faithful to keep us accountable and assist us on the journey of faith. It's helpful to have a brother or sister in Christ driving with you to help you through the difficult times, spot slippery situations, and lead you closer to Christ. Cultivate a friendship with a person or persons who will challenge you and hold you accountable to the resolutions you make in your life to grow in holiness. Look for holy friends in holy places and events. You may even consider asking a priest or youth minister to be your spiritual director whom you meet with regularly. Pray to God to bless you with such friends and mentors.

2. Spend time in groups: This is more in reference to dating couples, but it applies to those who are single as well. In order to establish chastity in your relationship, try to hang out with a group of friends rather than exclusively with each other. This helps you to be accountable for each other, and to look out for the well-being of your boy-friend or girlfriend rather than your own inter-ests. This will also help you set the foundation of your relationship on the rock of Christ.

3. Beware of boredom: As my youth minister told me when I was a teenager, "boredom is the Devil's playground." When our boredom is ex-treme, bad things tend to happen. Too much idle time can lead to bad thoughts and bad actions if we're not careful. Occupying yourself with some-thing like running, playing a sport, creating art, or reading a good book keeps your mind intact and free from wandering. If your mind does start to drift, get up and get busy with something. It's also important to moderate your time in front of the television, playing video games, or listening to music, and to examine how your media intake is affecting your relationship with Christ.

4. Pray, pray, and pray again: Without prayer, our union with Christ begins to weaken, and our tires begin to slip off the narrow road. Prayer keeps us grounded in Jesus. If prayer is something new for you, start small, maybe two minutes a day. Just call to mind Christ working in your life and ask for his assistance throughout the day, and add some-thing as simple as an Our Father or Hail Mary (see "Rest Area: Prayer" for more tips). When you face a temptation, say a short prayer right then to over-come it. Begin a relationship with your guardian angel, praying to be led away from the near oc-casions of sin and for help in overcoming sin. In addition, consider reading Scripture at least four times a week. Jesus speaks directly to you through his holy word! If you don't know where to start, begin with one of the four Gospels: either Matthew, Mark, Luke, or John.

5. Use sacramentals: Sacramentals are "any object set apart and blessed by the Church to [encourage] good thoughts and to increase devotion, and through these movements of the heart to remit venial sin."[13] For example, that Rosary dangling from the mirror above the car dash is a sacramental. It won't help you in your faith journey just by being there. You've got to use it! So take it down and clasp your fingers around the beads and pray, starting with just a decade. Other sacramentals include holy water, blessed salt, crucifixes, saint medals, and even the Sign of the Cross. These tools of the Faith remind us of the sacraments, and using them shows our desire to be closer to God. When we use sacramentals, we put on the "armor of God" (Eph 6:10–18).

Every day, we have to confront our adversary head-on, "For we are not contending against flesh and blood, but against the principalities, against the powers, against the world rulers of this present darkness, against the spiritual hosts of wickedness in the heavenly places" (Eph 6:12). The Devil's great sin was pride, so he tries to lead us in a similar direction. Therefore, humility is one great weapon against the powers of darkness. There is no greater act of humility than partaking in the Sacrament of Reconciliation. So if you find that you've slipped off the narrow road, drive your car to the nearest church and go to confession (check your parish bulletin online).

It is never easy to speak our sins aloud, but there is nothing more liberating than bringing our imperfections before the feet of Christ in the confessional. "The confession (or disclosure) of sins, even from a simply human point of view, frees us and facilitates our reconciliation with others. Through such an admission man looks squarely at the sins he is guilty of, takes responsibility for them, and thereby opens himself again to God and to the communion of the Church in order to make a new future possible" (CCC 1455). The greatest saints acknowledged that they were great sinners constantly in need of God's mercy. Pope Francis reminds us that "God never tires of forgiving us; we are the ones who tire of seeking his mercy."[14] It's important to remember as well that when we confess our sins, we are not confessing to the priest but to Christ. The priest acts *in persona Christi* (in the person of Christ) when he administers the sacrament. So it is God who forgives our sins, because only God can, and he does this through the apostolic ministry of the Church (CCC 1441). If it helps, imagine Jesus before you as you confess your sins to the priest, and pray that Jesus will truly speak to you through the confessor.

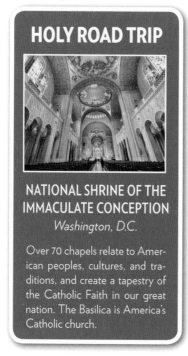

HOLY ROAD TRIP

NATIONAL SHRINE OF THE IMMACULATE CONCEPTION
Washington, D.C.

Over 70 chapels relate to American peoples, cultures, and traditions, and create a tapestry of the Catholic Faith in our great nation. The Basilica is America's Catholic church.

If you find that you have slipped into sin, pick yourself back up and seek God's forgiveness and grace. One of the tactics of the Devil is to try to lead us into despair. When we commit a sin, there can sometimes be a tendency to beat ourselves down and fall into despair. "I'm not worthy of God's love; I'm not worthy of God's mercy" are thoughts that may form in our minds. This is not of God. Jesus does not want us to deprecate ourselves to the point of turning away from him. When we fall, we need to acknowledge our sin, go to confession, and leave it in the past. If you are wrestling with a habitual sin or addiction, seek help and guidance from someone you can trust — but never despair. For that is, after all, the beauty of our Catholic Faith: we believe in a God who doesn't just forgive us "seven times, but seventy times seven" (Mt 18:22), or in other words, infinitely.

A priest friend once told me, "Sin is boring." It's easy to sin; it's more difficult to live lives of virtue, humility, and courage. The road to God is exciting because his ways challenge us and push us to become who he has created us to be. Seek a road that is smooth, not slick, by putting yourself in places conductive of God's grace and goodness! "Whatever is true, whatever is honorable, whatever is just, whatever is pure, whatever is lovely, whatever is gracious, if there is any excellence, if there is anything worthy of praise, think about these things" (Phil 4:8). If you do find yourself swerving toward sin and you lose control, remember that Jesus is there to remind you to pull the car over and get down on your knees!

QUESTIONS FOR REFLECTION

1. What is a near occasion of sin? What are some helpful personal steps to avoid slippery situations?
2. How does sin cause hurt in our lives and the lives of others?
3. What tools does the Church offer you on the (sometimes slippery) road of life to aid you on your way?

DETOUR
PURGATORY

Emily Borman

If any man's work is burned up, he will suffer loss, though he himself will be saved, but only as through fire.

1 CORINTHIANS 3:15

I vividly recall the first day I ever drove a car. My driving instructor, Mr. Henderson, said he is unlikely to forget that day, either. I was fifteen years old, almost sixteen, and I was nervous. In my home state, it was not legal to drive until you had your learner's permit, and you didn't receive your permit until day one of class. Since I am a rule follower, I had no driving experience. Zero. Zip. Nada. My two classmates were boasting about their driving skills, which made me all the more anxious. Steve grew up driving his grandfather's tractor every summer, while Kevin's father used to take him out driving on old country roads to practice.

Kevin was the first student to drive that day. After he had completed his turn, Mr. Henderson instructed him to pull into a parking lot so we could switch seats. Dread filled my mind and body. Nevertheless, I slipped into the front seat and repeated Mr. Henderson's instructions out loud: "Right-hand turn out of the parking lot, speed limit thirty-five, slow as I approach the intersection, left-hand turn at the light, yield to oncoming traffic, and stop if the light turns red."

As I got used to the gas pedal under my foot, the car lurched with fits and jerks. I entered the street and picked up a little speed, and thought to myself, "This isn't so hard after all!" My confidence was beginning to grow. When I approached the intersection, the light was green. Mr. Henderson reminded me to use my turn signal. There was no oncoming traffic, so I turned the wheel left, just as I did when playing video games. I forgot to slow down … at least I think that's what Mr. Henderson was shouting, but it was hard to hear him over the piercing screams coming from the boys in the backseat. We careened through the intersection directly toward a large US Post Office mailbox. Everyone's yelling and screaming made me panic even more, but I was somehow able to correct my steering just enough to avoid a collision. I was pretty happy to have missed the mailbox, but judging by the tone of Mr. Henderson's voice, happiness is not what he was feeling when he shouted, "You missed that mailbox by two centimeters! I saw my whole life pass before my eyes!"

Mr. Henderson never mentioned it, but I wonder if, when his whole life flashed before his eyes, he was contemplating what was next: heaven, purgatory, or hell? He seemed like a nice enough guy, but none of us is perfect. When we die, we each go through particular judgment and then proceed to heaven, purgatory, or hell. I think you'll agree: we want to go to heaven and not to hell. But what is purgatory?

Think of purgatory as a detour before you reach heaven. Have you ever come upon a big orange Detour sign that blocks off the road you intended to drive? Usually there is a black arrow pointing out a different road. If you follow the sign, you will still get to your destination; it's just going to take a little longer. If you make it to purgatory, you will definitely one day make it to heaven. There is no road from purgatory to hell. In

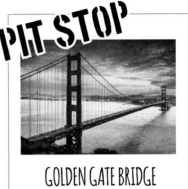

PIT STOP

GOLDEN GATE BRIDGE
San Francisco, California

Pull off at the Bridge Plaza to take a selfie with this iconic suspension bridge. This work of art/marvel of engineering is one of the Wonders of the Modern World.

purgatory, "all who die in God's grace and friendship, but still imperfectly purified, are indeed assured of their eternal salvation; but after death they undergo purification, so as to achieve the holiness necessary to enter the joy of heaven" (CCC 1030).

Purgatory is where we go to be purified of the temporal effects of our sins. Yes, even though Jesus already died for our sins, and even though you have gone to confession and been forgiven of your sins, you may still need to be purified. You see, sin has two consequences. One consequence is that sin separates us from God. The other consequence is called the "temporal punishment of sin," or the defects left by sin. A good contrite confession takes care of the first consequence by absolving our sin, so we are no longer separated from God or at risk of hell. Purgatory takes care of the second consequence by purifying the defects, so that we are ready to meet God face to face.

Usually when you are driving and face a detour,

there is a lot of roadwork happening. Imagine that when you were passing through the construction zone, you ended up driving over a nail, which then caused you to have a flat tire. Compare removing the nail to going to confession. The offending nail or sin has been removed. But you still have a hole in that tire that needs to be repaired. In the same way, every sin causes damage to us, and that damage needs to be repaired.

Before we meet God, it is vital that we are repaired or purified. Scripture tells us, "nothing unclean shall enter [heaven]" (Rv 21:27). The call to purify doesn't end there. Jesus tells us that we must be perfect (Mt 5:48)! Thankfully, Scripture also shows us that perfection is possible: "But you have come to Mount Zion and to the city of the living God, the heavenly Jerusalem ... and to a judge who is God of all, and to the spirits of just men made perfect" (Heb 12:22–23). Men and women can be made perfect. You can be made perfect. You can strive for it here on earth, which will help you bypass the detour of purgatory.

In Exodus, Moses asked to see God in his glory. God, knowing that Moses was not yet perfect and unprepared to see him in all his glory, protected him. God said to Moses, "you cannot see my face; for man shall not see me and live ... Behold, there is a place by me where you shall stand upon the rock; and while my glory passes by I will put you in a cleft of the rock, and I will cover you with my hand until I have passed by; then I will take away my hand, and you shall see my back; but my face shall not be seen" (Ex 33:20–23).

On another note of purgatory, did you notice that the last Scripture reference was from the Old Testament? People believed in praying for the dead even before Jesus was born. If there is any doubt in your mind about the existence or need for purgatory, check out the Councils of Florence and Trent. (By the way, an ecumenical council is a conference of bishops, who gather to discuss a matter of the Church). It was during those councils that Holy Mother Church formalized and confirmed what had been taught about purgatory since before the coming of Christ.

Are there some questions running through your mind? What is it like to be in purgatory? Will it hurt? The information we have leads us to believe it will probably involve purification through fire. According to Pope Benedict XVI, "In order to be saved, we personally have to pass through 'fire' so as to become fully open to receiving God and able to take our place at the table of the eternal marriage-feast."[15] Saint Paul writes, "[the person] will be saved, but only as through fire" (1 Cor 3:15). Saint Peter writes, "In this you rejoice, though now for a little while you may have to suffer various trials, so that the genuineness of your faith, more precious than gold which though perishable is tested by fire, may redound to praise and glory and honor at the revelation of Jesus Christ" (1 Pt 1:6–7).

ROADSIDE DISTRACTIONS

London Bridge

Lake Havasu City, Arizona

London Bridge was falling down ... so an American millionaire bought it and moved it stone by stone to Arizona. Just add water.

Saint Faustina is one of several saints who had visions of heaven, purgatory, and hell. She, too, mentions fire, and describes these visions in her diary.

I saw my Guardian Angel, who ordered me to
follow him. In a moment I was in a misty place
full of fire in which there was a great crowd of
suffering souls. They were praying fervently, but
to no avail, for themselves; only we can come to
their aid. The flames, which were burning them,
did not touch me at all. My Guardian Angel did
not leave me for an instant. I asked these souls
what their greatest suffering was. They answered
me in one voice that their greatest torment was
longing for God.[16]

Saint Francis de Sales, when he describes purgatory,
acknowledges that the pain of purgatory is worse than
anything we might feel on earth, but he points out that
we will feel great consolation in purgatory as well. Remember, the souls that make it to purgatory have freely and completely chosen God and will definitely make
it to heaven. Because of this, not only are they not able
to sin in purgatory, but they have no desire to; they are
completely resigned to God's will. This union with God,
although it is not yet perfect, gives great peace and consolation. Saint Francis de Sales's theory is that peace and
consolation lessen the torments of purgatory. He says,
"It is true that the torments are so great that the most
acute sufferings of this life bear no comparison to them;
but the interior satisfaction which is there enjoyed is
such that no prosperity nor contentment upon earth can
equal it. ... They wish to be there in the state wherein
God pleases, and as long as it shall please Him."[17]

You may be wondering now about your great-great-
grandparents, or maybe even a celebrity like Elvis who
has died. Are they suffering in purgatory? Is there any
way that you can help them? Yes, there is! Anyone on

earth can offer prayers and sacrifices for the souls in purgatory. Saint Faustina's vision reminds us of that. Our offerings can help alleviate their suffering. This teaching is based on Scripture, as we've seen, and the communion of saints that we profess in the Nicene Creed. The *Catechism* is also very clear on this: "'Therefore [Judas Maccabeus] made atonement for the dead, that they might be delivered from their sin.' From the beginning the Church has honored the memory of the dead and offered prayers in suffrage for them, above all the Eucharistic sacrifice, so that, thus purified, they may attain the beatific vision of God. The Church also commends almsgiving, indulgences, and works of penance undertaken on behalf of the dead" (CCC 1032).

So, yes, pray and sacrifice for all who have passed away. Don't worry about wasting prayers on someone who may already be in heaven. Prayers are never wasted. If the person you are praying for has already entered heaven, then your prayers will benefit another soul in purgatory. According to tradition, Saint Gertrude the Great experienced a revelation from our Lord in which he told her that, each time the following prayer was prayed sincerely, one thousand souls would be released from purgatory. If you pray this prayer forty-one times you could fill Chicago's Wrigley Field with all of the souls that would be released from purgatory!

Eternal Father, I offer Thee the Most Precious Blood of Thy Divine Son, Jesus, in union with the Masses said throughout the world today, for all the holy souls in purgatory, for sinners everywhere, for sinners in the universal Church, those in my own home and within my family. Amen.

Is purgatory starting to look better? Despite the flames, there is consolation. Despite the torment, people can pray and sacrifice to help the souls in purgatory. Those two attributes are great, but don't let them lure you away from your heavenly goal. Purgatory is not the destination; it's a detour. Keep your sights on heaven. If you aim for heaven and you miss, hopefully you'll land in purgatory. If you aim for purgatory and you miss, the consequences are eternally fatal. Purgatory may be a detour, but hell is driving off of a cliff into a fiery abyss with no chance for rescue. Yikes!

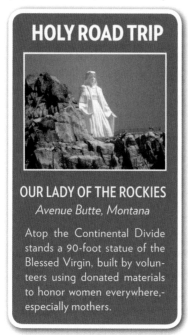

HOLY ROAD TRIP

OUR LADY OF THE ROCKIES
Avenue Butte, Montana

Atop the Continental Divide stands a 90-foot statue of the Blessed Virgin, built by volunteers using donated materials to honor women everywhere, especially mothers.

The best way to avoid purgatory is to focus on getting into heaven. We gain heaven by remaining in God's grace and friendship. Grace is not something that we can earn. God offers grace to us freely. He doesn't force it on us; we must choose it. We can choose it by frequently participating in the sacraments, particularly Communion and confession. Friendship with God involves time and love just like your other friendships. Friendship is about love, not fear. According to Saint Josemaría Escrivá, "You shouldn't want to do things to gain merit, nor out of fear of the punishments of purgatory. From now on, and always, you should make the effort to do everything, even the smallest things, to please Jesus."[18]

God gives us directions to help us reach heaven. Jesus said, "If you love me, you will keep my commandments" (Jn 14:15). He gave us the Bible (including the Ten Commandments), Holy Mother Church, and the sacraments. He wants us to keep his commandments, but he wants us to do it out of love and friendship for him, not out of fear. Some people think they can earn their way to heaven by following the commandments perfectly. If that were the case, none of us would get to heaven, because none of us is perfect. We all make mistakes. God knows that! We avoid purgatory and reach for heaven by choosing to follow God's directions because we love him. Then, when we get lost or make a wrong turn, we look at his directions and get back on track. We choose God's way again and again out of friendship and love. That's the road to heaven!

QUESTIONS FOR REFLECTION

1. What are the two consequences of sin?
2. How does a soul arrive in purgatory? What is the purpose of it? Should we aim for it?
3. How did Saint Faustina's and Saint Francis's visions of purgatory impact you?
4. How can we help souls in purgatory?

DEAD END
HELL

Miriam Marston

I have set before you life and death, blessing and curse; there-fore choose life, that you ... may live.

DEUTERONOMY 30:19

Dead End. It might not be the most cheerful road sign ever, yet it's quite useful. If we're trying to get to the right place, and avoid the roads that lead us away from our destination, this is a good road sign to heed. Where we are going should constantly be on our mind as we drive. In the same way, we have to keep our minds attuned to the spiritual destinations that are placed be-fore us.

Imagine that it's a Friday evening, and you are driv-ing to your friend's house. The windows are down and your new favorite song is on the radio, a great distrac-tion from the difficult week you've had. A few min-utes later, with a soda in hand, you flop down on your friend's couch with a big sigh and declare: "That was a week from hell!" By this, you might mean that you had five difficult tests to take, or a huge fight with a parent or sibling, or maybe you dented the family car. Whatever it was, it felt as though every bit of the plan you had sketched out for the week was opposed by the events of the last few days. Reality collided with your expectations; hence your unhappy refrain: "But that's not how things were supposed to go!"

Hell is not how things are supposed to go, in the sense that God has a loving plan for each one of us, and that plan doesn't involve spending an eternity as far away as possible from him. That "week from hell" that you had, when it felt like everything was falling apart and reality was detaching itself from your expectations and goals? Amplify that by infinity, and you've got a sense of what it would be like to exist perpetually with a "great chasm" (Lk 16:26) between you and everything holy. You were made for God.

As we're cruising along the roads of our lives, it would be problematic if (a) we refused to acknowledge any road signs indicating a dead end, or (b) we saw signs for dead ends everywhere (even where they didn't exist). When it comes to the discussion of hell, it can be tempting to slip into one of these two camps.

First up: the ignorers or deniers of hell. I know this group well, since some years ago I became quite clever at dodging the issue of hell. Like some of my peers, I couldn't seem to reconcile the belief in an all-good (or omnibenevolent) God with the belief that people could be "sent" to an unbearably hot and terrible place as punishment. But in a way, the possibility of hell reaffirms the all-loving and perfectly good nature of God. When the *Catechism* defines hell, the word "free" is used twice in just the first few sentences (CCC 1705). Free. It's almost surprising to find that word in such a context, but it's actually key to understanding what the Church teaches concerning hell.

Before going any further, here's a little piece of trivia: the Catholic Church has never declared anyone to be in hell. Because many people almost immediately jump to the question, "But what about Hitler?!" I hasten to add: The Church hasn't said that even Hitler is in hell. I bring this up now because any conversation on hell should include sufficient mention of the mercy of God.

"There's a wideness in God's mercy / Like the wideness of the sea."[19] These lyrics

PIT STOP

ST. LOUIS ARCH
St. Louis, Missouri

Look up from the ground below or take the tram inside to the very top for a breathtaking view. If you've got time, explore the museum's celebration of American pioneering spirit.

from an old hymn remind us that the mercy of God reaches further than we can imagine (this is excellent news for us!). So yes, while we see the awful deeds done by certain people in the past and present, we cannot truly know what is at work in the deepest regions of their souls. Ultimately, it is up to each soul to either accept or reject God. He does not choose hell for us; we do.

Each person at every point in history has been "endowed with freedom" (CCC 1705). From the start, God has known about the various risks attached to his splendid gift of free will. He knows that we are free to worship something or someone other than him. But in his perfect love, He couldn't give us anything less. The only other alternative would be the God-as-grand-puppeteer option. God could just tug this or that string, and we'd be prevented from straying too far off from him. But God won't drag you into heaven kicking and screaming. The *Catechism* is quite clear on this point: "we cannot be united with God unless we freely choose to love him" (CCC 1033). Think for a moment of the vows that are spoken at a wedding ceremony.

"Have you come here freely and without reservation to give yourselves to each other in marriage?" Naturally, the bride and groom each answer with an unambiguous "yes." They understand that they are making a free gift of themselves to each other, and no one forced them to come to the altar to make these vows.

Freedom works the other way too. Just as we freely embrace a loving relationship with God and so enter into his kingdom because there is nowhere else we'd rather be, so there has to be some provision or arrangement for those who, exercising their gift of freedom, ultimately — and utterly — reject God. Our heavenly Father would not be loving if he sidestepped free will and coerced such people into his presence. "Are there really people like that, though?" you might ask. But as painful as it might be to picture, there are those who, even after coming face to face with the truth of the Gospel, dig in their heels and say, "I have considered it, over and over, and I declare freely and resolutely: no — I do not desire this life that Christ offers me. I desire no other god in my world except me. I am the highest good and the end of everything. I — not Christ — am the Alpha and the Omega." They've just driven into a dead end!

So, just to be clear: God does not "send" someone to hell in the way that a parent "sends" a child to a time-out. People in hell have freely chosen to send themselves there. As I said, it's a bit painful to consider; and honestly, I wouldn't want you to spend *too* much time pondering the various punishments of hell. Many saints have had very terrifying visions of the torments below: Saint

Theresa of Avila, Saint Faustina, Saint John Bosco, and the Fatima children: Saint Francisco, Saint Jacinta, and Lucia. But it should be enough to ponder this: you can't find a lonelier or more isolated place than hell. It's a complete separation from love itself, from God. In hell, there is no fellowship, no possibility of communion, and not the tiniest shred of intimacy.

Besides the ignorers or deniers of hell, there are those who are convinced that only a small and elite group of men and women can make it to heaven. Their mantra is something along the lines of "I could never make it to heaven … I'll never be worthy enough, and hell is where I'm headed." Those who believe this are the people who see dead ends everywhere. This is related to something commonly referred to as scrupulosity, which tricks us into believing that eternal death is lurking behind even the smallest of sins. Our Lord Jesus Christ does not want us to lead lives of paranoia! He doesn't want us to think that hell is waiting there for us around every curve or bend in the road. Remember what he tells us: "I came that they may have life, and have it abundantly" (Jn 10:10). The abundant life isn't just about running away from hell. It's primarily about racing toward the splendors of the heavenly kingdom, and that involves boldly stepping into the business of being human and facing head-on the everyday realities of relationships, temptations, joys, and sorrows. Scrupulosity can have a paralyzing effect on the spiritual life. Getting stuck on this path would be like hiding in your house and never getting into your car to go anywhere, because you're afraid you'll fatally crash at any moment. Yes, you'd be alive, but would you really be living?

This is a good moment to make a pit stop and talk about two words: grave sin. It's also known as mortal sin (because such sins "deaden" our friendship with God). We don't want to leave this world in a state of grave sin, since doing so will land us stuck in a dead end, far away from our destination. When speaking of hell, Jesus said, "he who has ears, let him hear" (Mt 13:43), so we should probably lean in close to listen more carefully. He does not say that unrepentant sinners *might* be cast out of the heavenly kingdom. Rather, he is clear that the unrepentant soul who dies in grave sin will be thrown "into the furnace of fire, where there will be weeping and gnashing of teeth" (Mt 13:42). He promises eternal life to the righteous, and eternal punishment to the evildoers (cf. Mt 25:46). In choosing mortal sin, we are saying "no" to God. Living in sin, without repentance, is a way of rejecting God (CCC 1037). Mortal sins are most definitely dead ends. Nevertheless, God doesn't want anyone in hell. Scripture says, "The Lord is … forbearing toward you, not wishing that any should perish, but that all should reach repentance" (2 Pt 3:9).

ROADSIDE DISTRACTIONS

Hell, Michigan

Victim of really bad puns, it does in fact freeze over fairly often. Paradise, Michigan, is about five hours north.

"Hold on!" you might say. "What about purgatory? Can we aim for that?" Purgatory is not a final destination, so it's unwise to "aim" for it (not least of all because missing the mark could be deadly to your soul). Rather, it's a place of preparation, a detour on the direct route to heaven (see "Detour: Purgatory").

So what *does* it mean to commit a grave or mortal sin? Entire books have been written on this, but for our purposes it's enough to remember that "for a sin to be mortal, three conditions must together be met: [it] is sin whose object is *grave matter* and which is also committed with *full knowledge* and *deliberate consent*" (CCC 1857, emphasis added). If you are wondering what "grave matter" is, start with the Ten Commandments. So let's say the sin violates the Third Commandment, which includes the obligation to participate in Sunday Mass.

If the Catholic is *unaware* that missing Mass is a grave matter, that changes the heart of the matter. For example: I was baptized in a Methodist church and raised in a Catholic/Presbyterian household. I thought that the Catholic Mass and Protestant services were essentially the same thing, so there were times I didn't go to Sunday Mass. I eventually did learn the differences between the liturgies, and I was also taught that Catholics were obligated to go to Mass every Sunday. Therefore, if I were to intentionally skip Mass next Sunday, for no good reason, while knowing perfectly well what I was doing, I would be committing a grave sin. All the conditions are there: grave matter, full knowledge, and deliberate consent.

So let's pretend that you find yourself one day headed down a road that turns out to be a spiritual dead end. As you drive, you take a long, hard look in the mirror, and see the reflection of some mortal sins you've committed. At that moment, you realize those choices aren't going to make you happy in the long run. Because (and this is vital to remember) you were made for total and complete happiness, which is found only in Christ.

In such a case, there is no need to despair. The Church has been giving us a treasury of good news for over two thousand years now — the news that it is possible to get out of a dead end. But just as it might take a twelve-point turn to get out of a dead end, so it might take you a few turns to get out of a spiritual No Through Street. In the driving world, there's the chance of hitting someone's trash cans or frightening the neighborhood cat with sudden, jerky movements of the car. There's no doubt about it: turning around in order to get out of a dead end can feel pretty awkward. That goes for the spiritual life as well. All that shuffling around in your seat during the Sacrament of Reconciliation? The lengthy litany of Hail Marys and Our Fathers for your penance? All part of the awkward turning around. But every moment is absolutely worth it, when you find yourself once again on the right road. In the words of C. S. Lewis, "I do not think that all who choose wrong roads perish; but their rescue consists in being put back on the right road. A [mathematical] sum can be put right: but only by going back until you find the error and working it afresh from that point, never by simply going on."[20]

If you insist on accelerating into a dead end, the odds are fairly high that you're just going to hit a wall or smash into someone's living room. It won't work, and it definitely won't bring you joy — only further damage, and costly damage at that. Replacing a totaled car is no small thing, after all. So turning around really is the best option. There is even a special word for this turning around, the turning away from sin: *metanoia*, the Greek word for conversion. This possibility of conversion gives us great hope when we're stuck in a dead end. Jesus Christ himself gives us a fairly straightforward prescription for those times when we're stuck: "repent, and believe in the gospel" (Mk 1:15). The word "repent" can sound heavy and daunting. Maybe that's because it's frequently associated with John the Baptist, who is often depicted as being somewhat wild, eating locusts and yelling in the desert. But the words "repent and believe in the gospel" are incredibly joyful and hopeful words. They are an invitation to *metanoia*.

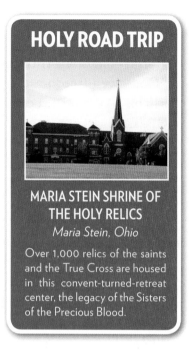

HOLY ROAD TRIP

MARIA STEIN SHRINE OF THE HOLY RELICS
Maria Stein, Ohio

Over 1,000 relics of the saints and the True Cross are housed in this convent-turned-retreat center, the legacy of the Sisters of the Precious Blood.

And come to think of it, a little friendly yelling from others might not do us much harm. If you've ever had the experience of having to maneuver your car in or out of a tight spot, you'll know how helpful it is to have someone outside, saying, "Stop! Okay, go a little bit to the left … no wait, that's too far … turn a little to the right, okay, stop, you're good!"

You are not alone. You might think that you're completely on your own, but that's just another trick of the Evil One to keep you away from heavenly union with God. So don't be afraid to ask the saints for help. Appeal to your guardian angel and to Mary, our Mother. Turn to your family and friends to hold you accountable to the good laws that have been written on our hearts. After all, they'd probably let us know if we were violating the laws in the driver's manual, right?

Avoiding a dead end, and staying on the narrow road, is a matter of daily decisions. "We [live in a world] where every road, after a few miles, forks into two, and each of those into two again, and at each fork you must make a decision."[21] We can choose eternal life or death at many points during an average week. This isn't scrupulosity, but rather Christian realism. Instead of paralyzing us, our God-given freedom allows us to act decisively and charitably. We can start each day with a very simple petition: "Lord, grant me the grace to be even a little better today than I was yesterday. Help my words to be more tender, my faith to be stronger, and my love to be truer." Choosing heaven over hell begins with our small choices. Maybe you'll reach a fork in the road that tempts you to gossip about someone. Try staying silent and praying for the person instead. If someone is unfortunate enough to be at the center of a rumor, then they probably need the extra prayers anyway. Feeling the urge to eat too much? Turn away from gluttony by putting down the excessive food and feel the satisfaction of self-mastery by small sacrifices (fasting isn't just for Lent). We often hear that no battle is too great when Christ is at our side. I agree! The same God who made heaven and earth has adopted us as his sons and daughters, and we should draw tremendous strength and courage from that. Indeed, no battle is too great, but I should add: no victory is too small. Conquering even the most seemingly mild of sins will help us steer clear of those dead ends.

Let's close with these powerful words from an ancient Holy Saturday homily by Saint John Chrysostum: "O death, where is your sting? O hell, where is your victory?"[22]

These are triumphant and hopeful words to anyone who hears them. Through his death and resurrection, Jesus Christ has overcome the grave and conquered sin. He stands at the entrance of every dead end, with his hand outstretched, inviting us to turn around. We shouldn't be afraid to roll down our windows and ask him for directions. His words can only lead us home to heaven.

QUESTIONS FOR REFLECTION

1. How do people drive into the dead end of hell?
2. What is scrupulosity, and how can it affect your spiritual life?
3. What is grave sin? Why is it a dangerous state for your soul? How do you get out of a spiritual dead end?
4. What is the Greek word for turning away from sin, and what does it in entail?

REST AREA
PRAYER

Jennessa Terraccino

You who seek God, let your hearts revive.

PSALM 69:32

When I moved from the Washington, D.C., area to Boston, I filled a rental truck with everything I owned and started driving up Route 95. The trip seemed manageable at an estimated eight hours, but the truck reached a thrilling speed of 55 mph before it got shaky. Plus, the alignment was off, so driving became a tug-of-war game between the steering wheel and me. With merely a basic radio, the truck didn't have much of a road-trip soundtrack to offer besides its own symphony of sounds, the cars zooming past, and my internal complaints. The hours and the road stretched on before me. When I entered New York City traffic, my wheels were down to a crawl, and the tolls were hitting my wallet hard! Despite the hungry rumble in my stomach, and the thought that I should probably not have drunk so much water, I had it in my head that if I didn't stop I'd get to my destination sooner. Despite my stiff and sluggish body, strained eyes, and road boredom, I stubbornly forged ahead, passing by rest area after rest area. On the fuel gauge, that little orange arrow on my dashboard was approaching the big "E." I was in desperate need of a break, and if I kept forging ahead, I'd soon be out of gas. Reluctantly, I stopped at a rest area and learned a valuable lesson. It is amazing what a little R&R can do for a driver, and fuel for a truck! The remaining miles of the drive felt more doable, and I actually enjoyed the final hours on the road. The break may have added a few minutes to my trip, but I was in better spirits.

Often in life, our hearts are on empty, and we push through, running on fumes. Refusing to pull over to a rest area leaves us tired, directionless, and burned out. Most of us are convinced we don't have time to stop and pray. If we are being honest, God often is at the bottom of our very full schedule (if he is even on it at all). Like my moving truck's steering wheel, we are often pulled in many directions, usually away from God and toward the world's attractions. This is exactly how my faith used to be. Yes, I went to Mass, but that was it. I had a motionless and emotionless faith, putting in the minimum while distracting myself with my busyness. There was always something on my heart: a gentle whisper that beckoned me to something deeper, a feeling that I should pray more, an invitation.

But how do we begin to pray? A great place to start your prayer journey, and find much-needed rest, is with simple and even quick morning and evening prayers. Indeed, the best habit you can foster is when your eyes peel open in the morning, do a ninja maneuver out of bed and onto your knees, and thank Jesus for one more day. Next, call upon the third person of the Trinity, the Holy Spirit. Ask him to guide you in prayer and in your day. "The Church invites us to call upon the Holy Spirit every day, especially at the beginning and the end of every important action" (CCC 2670). You can go for an old antiphon such as "Come, Holy Spirit, fill the hearts of your faithful and kindle in them the fire of your love." Or you can use your own prayerful words

PIT STOP

SAN ANTONIO RIVER WALK
San Antonio, Texas

Along the Riverwalk, you'll find five Spanish colonial missions, the Alamo, restaurants, shopping, museums, and, if you go at the right time, the colorful spring Fiesta.

to the Holy Spirit. Moreover, you should do a morning offering to Jesus so that all you do can be for his glory.

At night, consider doing a prayer of thanksgiving for your daily blessings and an examination of conscience: an authentic calling to mind of our actions, thoughts, and words from the day, humbling ourselves and asking for God's forgiveness for all of our sins.

Morning and night prayer are just the bookends of a relationship with God our Father. Yes, you read that correctly: a relationship! Prayer is not robotics. Pope Francis tells us "our prayer cannot be reduced to an hour on Sundays. It is important to have a daily relationship with the Lord."[23] You may not feel it yet, but prayer is about the heart; it is a true love for and from our heavenly Father. I love how Saint Thérèse of Lisieux describes prayer: "For me, prayer is a surge of the heart; it is a simple look turned toward heaven; it is a cry of recognition and of love, embracing both trial and joy" (CCC 2558). I love that word "surge," which implies movement such as a rising up, an increase, a rush, a burst of feeling, and an electrical current. That sounds intense, doesn't it? Prayer can do all that to the heart? Yes, it can reinvigorate and revitalize you if you rest in it!

Scripture invites us to more, proclaiming, "You who seek God, let your hearts revive" (Ps 69:32). Prayer sounds like spiritual CPR for hearts in need of rest and recovery. "Prayer is the life of the new heart. It ought to animate us at every moment. But we tend to forget Him who is our life and our all" (CCC 2697). You are God's beloved daughter or son. He wants to love you, and be loved by you. Open yourself to such a relationship; pull over and take a rest in Christ. Refuel your heart!

Many of us have spent years of religion classes learning a whole lot about the Trinity: the Father, Son, and Holy Spirit. Yet, many of us know a lot *about* God, but do not actually know God personally. Even the enemy knows a lot about God. Anyone would think it silly to attend guitar lessons week after week but never actually pick up a guitar and play during or after the lesson. That person would profess to know a lot about playing guitar, but would not actually have the ability to do so.

God is not just something to know about; he is not a list of characteristics. The Gospel isn't a collection of fables, and prayer isn't a mere duty. However, if we fail to pray, God will never be real to us, we will never truly know him, and we will never find and feel that intimacy for which we were made. Our deepest need is to be loved, and often we search for that love in every other place and person except for in the Persons of the Trinity. "[I pray] that Christ may dwell in your hearts through faith; that you ... know the love of Christ which surpasses knowledge, that you may be filled with all the fulness of God" (Eph 3:17, 19).

So, once you have committed to morning and night prayer, go a little deeper. There are many types of prayer, ways to pray, and places to pray. One type is adoration, which is "the first attitude of man acknowledging that he is a creature before his Creator. It exalts the greatness of the Lord who made us" (CCC 2628). Thus, adoration takes humility. When you genuflect or kneel before the King of Glory, your posture reflects your meekness before the Almighty. "At the name of Jesus every knee shall bow, in heaven and on earth and under the earth, and every tongue confess that Jesus Christ is Lord, to the glory of God the Father" (Phil 2:10–11). Besides kneeling being a sign of adoration, I find it really helps me focus while praying. Kneeling separates prayer from any other action that we do throughout our day. During the day, I sit, I walk, I lie down, but I really do not find myself kneeling for any other reason than to pray. Oddly enough, I find that it can be a posture of rest as well, as I collapse body and soul into the arms of God. Thus, the posture of our bodies truly orients us toward heaven, aiding our ability to converse with Jesus. Certainly, kneeling is not the only prayer posture, but it's a very helpful and humbling one.

Then there's Eucharistic adoration. "The Eucharist is the heart and summit of the Church's life" (CCC 1407). As Catholics we believe that the Eucharist is the Body, Blood, Soul, and Divinity of Jesus. Not only do we receive Jesus in communion at Mass, but he dwells in our churches as well, because the Blessed Sacrament is always present in the tabernacle. "It is highly fitting that Christ should have wanted to remain present to his Church in this unique way. Since Christ was about to take his departure from his own in his visible form, he wanted to give us his sacramental presence ... he wanted us to have the memorial of the love with which he loved us 'to the end,' even to the giving of his life. In the Eucharistic presence he remains mysteriously in our midst as the one who loved us and gave himself up for us" (CCC 1380). Thus, we should open ourselves up to receive this love from our living God by adoring him and receiving him in the Most Holy Sacrament of the Altar.

ROADSIDE DISTRACTIONS

The World's Largest Collection of Smallest Versions of Largest Things

Lucas, Kansas

Say that ten times fast. This mobile museum is full of things like a tiny souvenir replica of the Largest Ball of Twine.

The most intimate form of Eucharistic adoration is exposition, which means the Eucharist is taken from the tabernacle and placed in a monstrance. The Latin word for monstrance translates "to expose to view" or "to show." Traditionally, a monstrance will be gold, and will have a long stem that meets a round solar design, and within the sunburst will be a round window where the consecrated Host rests to be adored.

When you go to adore Jesus, you can do any number of things, from just simply sitting with Jesus, gazing at him, praying some favorite prayers, singing praise, reading Scripture, lifting up intentions, or even diving into the deep mystery of the Eucharist (cf. Gn 3:22; Ex

12:1–24; Sir 24:21; Jn 6:27–58, Mt 26:26–28; 1 Cor 10:18; 1 Cor 11:27–29; Acts 2:42; Rv 2:7). Making regular visits to adore Jesus will definitely grow your prayer life. It may be hard to sit quietly at first, but if you sit long enough, Jesus' love will push through your "antsyness" and distraction, and you will feel the warmth of his presence and be able to rest in him. Welcome the silence, and listen to God.

The great Saint John Damascene described prayer as "the raising of one's mind and heart to God or the requesting of good things from God" (CCC 2559). Now, we have already talked about the importance of engaging our hearts in prayer, so let's focus on the latter part of Saint John's definition, which is petition. It is important to ask our Father in heaven to supply us with the needs of our family, our friends, ourselves, and the universal Church. "We have confidence before God; and we receive from him whatever we ask, because we keep his commandments and do what pleases him" (1 Jn 3:21–22).

Sometimes we tend to ask God for things in the far future. This is not a bad thing to do, but I think it prevents us from seeing God's hand at work in the present moment of our lives. It is important to petition God even in small matters. "When we share in God's saving love, we understand that *every need* can become the object of petition" (CCC 2633). God wants what is best for us, so he will not supply us with something that is not his will. God is not a genie: he is a Father who is all-loving and has the best in mind for you. Let go of all of your needs, worries, thoughts, and desires in prayer. Bring it all to Jesus! "Have no anxiety about anything, but in everything by prayer and supplication with thanksgiving let your requests be made known to God" (Phil 4:6).

Moreover, there is also something to be said about perseverance in prayers of petition. In the Gospel of Mark, we see a woman who asked Jesus to cast a demon out of her daughter. At first Jesus did not respond to her request, but she asked again. Eventually, he responded to her determined efforts and healed her daughter (cf. Mk 7:24–30). Jesus also tells us that in prayer he will answer us lovingly. We're holding ourselves back when we don't pray. Let go of the brakes, and pray from your heart! "Ask, and it will be given to you; seek, and you will find; knock and it will be opened to you. For every one who asks receives, and he who seeks finds, and to him who knocks it will be opened. Or what man of you, if his son asks him for bread, will he give him a stone? ... If you then, who are evil, know how to give good gifts to your children, how much more will your Father who is in heaven give good things to those who ask him" (Mt 7:7–11).

In all things, it is important to give thanks and praise to God, whether you are thanking him for answering a prayer, or just recognizing the many blessings he has bestowed upon you without your even asking. So often we get bogged down in negativity. But honestly, if we take some time to think about what we are thankful for, we will find a lot for which to offer thanks (such as, "Wow, that fall foliage I am driving through is really beautiful!"). Jesus is blessing you right now; meditate on those blessings, and thank him for them. In Scripture, we see Jesus perform many miraculous healings. At one point he cleanses ten lepers, but only one leper comes back to thank him. It is so easy to ask, so easy to receive, and so easy to forget to offer thanks. Be the one who returns to offer thanks to Christ (cf. Lk 17:11–19). Offer Jesus a "sacrifice of praise" (Heb 13:15) with your words (or through music) using some of his many titles, such as: Rock, Mighty God, Lamb of God, Alpha and Omega, Prince of Peace, Light of the World, Living Bread, Good Shepherd, My Lord, My God, and My Redeemer.

Another form of prayer is intercession. This type of prayer is very important because it calls us out of ourselves. "In intercession, he who prays looks 'not only to his own interests, but also the interests of others,' even to the point of praying for those who do him harm" (CCC 2635). We are the Body of Christ, and part of the communion of saints: on earth, in purgatory, and in heaven. Prayer connects us and sustains us all. We pray for others while they pray for us. On the road of life, we must look to see the needs of others: our sick grandmother, our struggling neighbor, our friend who is going through a hard time, the homeless, the imprisoned, those suffering in purgatory, our priests, and whomever else we encounter who needs prayer.

As seen, there are many types of prayer, and within those types, prayer can take on a variety of forms. There is freelance or spontaneous prayer — simply lifting up your own words from your heart to God. However, if you are having a hard time coming up with your own words, start with some vocal prayers that you know, such as the Our Father, Hail Mary, or Glory Be. When you choose these prayers, pray them slowly, and really think about the words. You can also link an intention to each vocal prayer. In time, you will be able to pair these more structured prayers with a personal dialogue.

As you mature in prayer, turn to a deeper form of prayer: that of meditation. This form of prayer "engages thought, imagination, emotion, and desire" (CCC 2708). Get caught up in the life of Christ through meditation. You can do this by praying the Rosary, where you call upon a variety of Gospel scenes and dwell in the mystery. You can also do this by reading Scripture (a form of prayer called *Lectio Divina*) and pausing to soak in the story and allow it to simmer in your heart, waiting for a word or verse to speak to you directly. "Meditation is like a conversation between you and your best friend about a really good movie you've just seen. Talking about the movie helps you both to reveal more about yourselves and learn something, and the sharing deepens the connection between the two of you."[24]

Another way to go deeper is to picture yourself and Jesus somewhere: walking on the beach, sitting under a tree near a creek, standing together on a mountaintop. Where do you find yourself with Christ? Pick a place that feels comfortable to you. On the busy road of life, allow this to be your oasis, a rest area, and your very own special dwelling place with Jesus. Return there often to converse with Christ or just to linger in his presence. This form of prayer will open doors to contemplation, which is like "the last moment you saw your best friend, right before you moved away. You looked at each other, and there was really nothing to say. No words could express how you felt. All you could do was just be there, deep in your friendship and all that it was at that moment."[25]

In order to foster a life of prayer, there are three things you must do. First, make time. Stop trying to "fit God in" and just pull over the car. "Somehow, you always find time, in the midst of your crazy, terribly busy schedule, for the things that are important to you."[26] Is God a priority? This leads us into the second thing you must do: commit to prayer. Commitment and time go together. Make time to pray, and then stick with it. You won't always feel like praying, you might forget one day, and some days will be better than others — but stick with it! You must choose it, and in choosing to pray, you are choosing a relationship with Jesus. In addition to structured prayer time, lift your heart to Jesus throughout your day. In Scripture, Saint Paul reminds us to "pray constantly" (1 Thes 5:17). Glance toward heaven for a second, tell Jesus that you love him, ask him to go before you in occurrences throughout your day, ask him to have mercy on you, and tell him you trust in him. This will help you remain in the presence of God always. Third, find a place where you can pray well (your rest area). This doesn't have to be a church, though that is always a good place to pray. Your designated place could be in your room in front of a crucifix. If you don't have such a place in your room or home, consider making one. It doesn't have to be elaborate. Having some kind of small sacred space where you can retreat to and pray will be very helpful.

HOLY ROAD TRIP

SHRINE OF THE MOST BLESSED SACRAMENT
Hanceville, Alabama

The focal point of this overwhelmingly beautiful church and grounds is the seven-foot-tall monstrance, where pilgrims are invited to join the Poor Clares of Perpetual Adoration in prayer.

Overall, there are many battles in prayer. Why is prayer a battle? Because the enemy wants to keep you from God. He will work to "distract you, entice you, seduce you, and argue you away from prayer," and "He doesn't want you to be in touch with God who loves you passionately, wants the best for you, and gives you the strength to find what is best. He doesn't want you to be in touch with the good, the true, and the beautiful, and the holy."[27] His weapons come through your thoughts: *I don't have time to pray; I am too tired to pray; I prayed yesterday; God doesn't hear me when I pray; God never answers me; prayer is boring; I'd rather watch my favorite show and unwind, etc.* The enemy will also seek to distract you before you pray and when you pray. When you become distracted and recognize the distraction, turn back to your prayer. You might find yourself fighting other battles in prayer, such as dryness, laziness, lack of faith, and more. Personally, when I feel the least like praying, those are the moments I need Jesus most.

On life's journey, do not allow yourself to pass by the rest area where you will find the opportunity to rejuvenate through prayer. As much as we'd like to believe, we can't do it on our own. Just as your body and mind need a break after a long, strenuous drive, our soul thirsts for Christ on the road of life (cf. Ps 42:2). Amid our busy lives, Jesus beckons us to himself, saying "Come to me … I will give you rest" (Mt 11:28).

QUESTIONS FOR REFLECTION

1. Do you feel called to go deeper in your spiritual life? Why do you think Saint Thérèse called prayer the "surge of the heart?"
2. What is one type of prayer that is new to you, and that you feel drawn to pursue?
3. Why do you think it is important to have a daily relationship with Jesus? How can you make your prayers more personal and heartfelt?
4. Why is prayer often a battle? What are some of the enemy's tactics to keep you from stopping for a spiritual rest?

WINDING ROAD
THE HIGHS AND LOWS OF LIFE

Kimberly Cook

In all your ways acknowledge him, and he will make straight your paths.

PROVERBS 3:6

The road I chose to take was a winding one. Though I had grown up in a Catholic household, our family had fallen away from the Faith shortly before my formative high school years. Consequently, I felt most abandoned and distant from God at a time when I needed faith and hope more than anything. Searching to "find myself" led me down some dark and winding roads occupied by shady characters. Even in our middle-class town, many of my friends (and their parents) were using drugs, experimenting with their sexuality, and propelling themselves into reckless lifestyles. I too was rebellious. For the first time in my life, like many other teens, I encountered heavy topics such as death and suicide. My faith, morals, and philosophies were challenged; and when put to the test, they withered. There no longer seemed to be a clear-cut right and wrong. Everything suddenly seemed to fall somewhere in the gray.

Answers were relative to the situation at hand, and they were always dictated by emotions. I had embraced the idea that there were no absolute truths, and that meant no absolute anything (see "One Way: Truth and Life"). This included no absolute certainty that there was even a God, that there was life after death, or that my life had any purpose at all. The world of carefree freedom that I had been searching for turned out to be a dead-end road (see "Dead End: Hell").

While this whirlwind blew around me from the outside, something equally unsettling went on within me. I was experiencing many new feelings and emotions, hormones that seemed to have a life of their own, and ultimately a depression that set in like a dark cloud in my soul. I looked around but could not find a friend who had that spark of hope that I was longing for; someone I could confide in, who would point me toward the light at the end of the winding road. While God was always in my rearview mirror, I certainly hadn't given him control of my life's wheel, or even a spot as copilot. Yet I couldn't quite take my eyes off him, in the same way that a novice driver can't stop glancing at the cars creeping up behind them. I glanced more than ever at the beckoning God in my rearview mirror, intrigued through the noise and chaos by his "still small voice" (1 Kgs 19:12). It was ultimately my choice to hear and to follow.

God desires to guide us through the twists and turns of any dark, winding road we end up on. Sometimes, to accomplish this, he works through people. Perhaps you have encountered one of these people who possess the spark of hope for which you long. The people are few and far between who are lights in the darkness (see "Blind Pedestrian: Spiritual Sight"). These gentle souls shine so brightly with the light of Christ that you cannot help but be drawn to them, like a moth to a flame. You want what they have: the peace, the joy, the confidence in something greater than oneself. Sometimes these people are just flickering flames that you briefly encounter on the winding road, and other times they remain in your life to set it ablaze! (See "Fire Engine Crossing: Evangelization.")

PIT STOP

SPACE NEEDLE
Seattle, Washington

From the top floors, which include the world's first and only revolving glass floor, you'll get a spectacular view of Seattle's skyline and the surrounding mountains, bay, and islands.

There is something authentic about them that you recognize almost immediately: their capacity to love. These people are gifts from God on your journey toward him. They are road signs guiding you through the winding road to the straight one, the path that will bring you to your greatest happiness.

I can remember one particular "flickering flame" named Abigail. My friend Kate and I had just gotten summer jobs at a golf course. We worked mostly in the kitchen, but occasionally would go joyriding across the green on a swerving golf cart. We were loud and reckless, and should have scared the pants off of the bright and cheery Abigail. Yet I remember that despite my every effort to dress and act "dark," Abigail brought out the "light" in me. I felt no judgment or difference between us, and I actually liked being around her (which I couldn't say about many other people at that time). Naturally, I sought out the root of her joy, which led to a deep conversation about her Catholic Faith. It took courage for her to speak with such conviction on topics that were hotter than the stoves surrounding us. I took the safer route, nonchalantly throwing in the fact that I was also Catholic, but quickly adding that I wasn't really sure what I believed yet. Then I held my breath and waited for the lecture, but it never came.

Abigail simply shared her own authentic passion for the Faith and how it brought her great joy. I couldn't believe that this high school girl was *freely* choosing to go to Mass, read the Bible, and love and serve God. Where was the rebellion in that? The thing I couldn't explain, though, was the power of her passion. It shined; it radiated; it could be seen like a house overdecorated with Christmas lights from miles away on my winding road. She was happy. She had peace. Meanwhile, I was miserable.

Abigail's flame ignited a spark in my life. The summer passed and our work shifts rarely aligned. After those few short months, I never saw her again. I wish I could find her now and tell her how much her simple witness affected me, changed me, and ultimately pointed me in the direction of Christ, whom I so desperately needed. Thank you, Abigail, wherever you are.

Fast forward a few months. It was hard to concentrate on the wintry, winding, backcountry road. My hands clutched the wheel and my back hurt from sitting so far forward in the driver's seat. Snow was falling, so it was hard to tell when the road would bend and curve next. Even though I had driven this road many times in the past, the snow and ice made it completely unfamiliar. I felt trapped, halfway between home and my destination. As I rounded the next bend at the speed of an injured snail, I saw two cars in the embankment at the bottom of the hill I was approaching. My danger radar went off, but it was too late. My wheels were already following the other cars' tracks on the black ice.

As my vehicle gained momentum down the icy hill, time inside the car seemed to slow down. I tried all the driver-safety techniques I had learned. Pumping my brakes was useless. Turning the steering wheel in any direction did nothing to change the direction my car was headed — right into the other two cars in the embankment. As I watched the embankment rush closer and closer to the hood of my car, I surrendered to the helpless feeling that came over me.

In that moment, I whispered a simple and desperate plea to Jesus for help and protection. It's funny how we cry out to God in our moments of greatest fear, no matter how distant we have been from him. As Scripture says, "In my distress I called upon the Lord; to my God I cried for help. From his temple he heard my voice, and my cry to him reached his ears" (Ps 18:6). I wish I could say because of that prayer my car miraculously swerved out of the tracks and somehow centered itself back on the road. I can't say that. What I can say, however, is that by the grace of God, my car did slow down before barely bumping the truck in front of me. Amazingly, there was no significant damage to either vehicle, and thankfully no one else came barreling around that bend while my car was stuck. As many teenage girls would do, I called my dad to come rescue me, and he did. But, my Father in heaven had rescued me—and had begun a much bigger rescue in my life. He was determined to rescue my soul from the winding road it was traveling.

After my snowy and scary car incident, the Lord's fight continued through another encounter. When my high school boyfriend told me that I *had* to meet his boss, I thought it strange how excited and convinced he was about it. I reluctantly agreed. As I walked through the front door of the graphic design office, my pink hair and rocker-chick clothes made a statement long before I opened my mouth. I will never forget the warmth with which Mr. Charles greeted me, lovingly taking my hand. His whole face seemed to light up, and he never stopped smiling or took his eyes off of me as we talked. It was as if he had been waiting for me to walk through that door his whole life. There was something very special about him, even mystical. I was intrigued. It was almost as if his was the face of Christ.

I came to realize that Mr. Charles had a beautiful gift: he was filled with the love of Christ. Because of this, he was able to read my heart and bring to light hidden struggles that I had shared with no one. I surprised even myself by starting to weep almost instantly as we began speaking. I will never forget the moment that he looked at me and told me that I was beautiful. It was as if Jesus was speaking through him. For the first time in a long time, someone actually meant those words; and for the first time in a long time, I truly believed them. This was the love of Christ — a love I had longed for, but had lost along the way. This encounter was the first of many, as Christ's love began to change me in radical ways. In him, I became joyful. This time when I took the wheel, God was no longer in my rear view; he was very much in control. I was living authentically.

You may find that your own life is a winding road. You will experience highs and lows, peaks and valleys, traffic jams and fender benders. Yet there are also many beautiful scenic views, in which Mother Nature spoils you with her splendor around every turn and bend. You never know what God has waiting for you just around the next corner, "for the Lord your God is a merciful God; he will not fail you" (Dt 4:31). Remember, his plans for you are filled with hope! God is with you in the barren valleys when you cry out to him in despair, and he is with you on the mountain-tops when your heart sings to him in joy.

ROADSIDE DISTRACTIONS

International Cryptozoology Museum

Portland, Maine

More than just statues of Bigfoot and the Loch Ness Monster fill this unique attraction. Here you can find "rare, one-of-a-kind scientific, zoological specimens."

In your life, whether you are hitting a high or a low, it is important to surround yourself with people who radiate the love of Christ. Look to encounter your own Abigail or Mr. Charles on your winding road. Ask Jesus to send someone. After all, in Jesus' darkest moments, Simon was sent to aid Christ in carrying his cross (cf. Mt 27:32), and Saint Veronica was drawn to wipe the face of Christ on the *Via Dolorosa* (Way of Sorrow). When the way looks hopeless, God is still present, often working through others. Groups at church are a great way to find those walking the talk; start with your parish youth group. No matter where you are on the winding road, you are welcome.

After trying a million wrong ways to get to him, I found that what he really desired from me was humility and purity. As Saint Padre Pio said, "Humility and purity are the wings which carry us to God and make us almost divine. Remember: that a bad man who is ashamed of the wrong things he is doing, is nearer to God than a good man who blushes at doing the right thing."[28] So I put the car in reverse and set out to find happier trails. What I wanted more than anything was to repair the broken and failing relationship I had with my parents. I wanted to regain their trust so that I could share with them what I had found: the joy of Christ and the richness of the Catholic Church. This became my fervent prayer, and I worked every day to bite my tongue and to answer negative remarks with positive ones. I forgave the hurt and learned to love, even if love was not always returned. To my surprise, I found that this really worked! Hearts were warmed and changed through this constant outpouring of love.

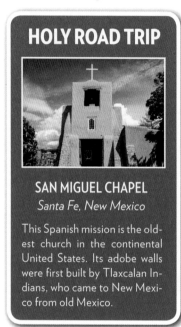

HOLY ROAD TRIP

SAN MIGUEL CHAPEL
Santa Fe, New Mexico

This Spanish mission is the oldest church in the continental United States. Its adobe walls were first built by Tlaxcalan Indians, who came to New Mexico from old Mexico.

I chose to go to a Catholic college called Franciscan University. I knew that I needed to be surrounded by others who had found what I had, at least until I learned to grow my own wings in the Faith. Little by little I changed, and little by little my family changed. My parents fully embraced the Faith, and our relationship became one of deep love and respect for one another.

Ultimately, I found the true meaning of freedom down the winding road: the freedom to choose God. I found that by free will we shape our own road — that is, our life. With Christ, that road can be a lot better to travel; we simply need to embrace him. "In all your ways acknowledge him, and he will make straight your paths" (Prv 3:6). I pray that if God is in your rearview mirror, you might consider pulling over and at least giving him a ride, to hear what he has to say. If you are already on the "straight and narrow road," grab a passenger.

QUESTIONS FOR REFLECTION

1. Do you feel like you are traveling on a straight or winding road right now? Why? How can you ultimately shape your own road?
2. How can you allow Christ's love to change you in radical ways?
3. On the winding road, how can you surround yourself with people who are living for Christ?
4. Why do you think humility and purity are important virtues to possess?

YIELD
SERVING OTHERS IN CHRISTIAN CHARITY

Allison Gingras

The Son of man came not to be served but to serve.

MATTHEW 20:28

O nce you've had your driver's license a while, you typically believe your days of learning how to drive are over. But I learned that is not always true. As long as you are alive and open to them, there are always opportunities to learn. Such a chance came when I was driving my friend, a retired state trooper, to a parish event. The trip required me to yield at the end of a ramp onto a very busy highway. I had done this maneuver hundreds of times before, and I felt confident that I knew what I was doing. As I approached the bottom of the on-ramp, I slowed down to be sure it was safe to enter. My friend very adamantly, yet politely, encouraged me not to stop but to put on my blinker (or as we say here in New England, "blinkah"). Next, she directed me to stay in the merge lane until it was safe to move into the travel lane.

To yield to the traffic meant that I had to wait until it was safe for me to enter onto the highway, and that I had to give way to those already there. This takes the virtue of patience, as well as being able to put others' needs before one's own. To accomplish this, I needed to use the extra lane provided. In life, God often gives us these same safe trails to traverse before we enter into new paths of life, especially as we are entering into a deeper relationship with him. Just like merging onto a busy road, we must be aware not only of where we are going, but also of who else is on this road with us. The ability to listen and pay attention to others, alongside an openness to allowing the Holy Spirit to move in your life, unfolds a different definition of the word *yield* — to produce or provide. In my own life, I've discovered that my willingness to submit to the authority of others, especially God, and my willingness to serve others has yielded a bounty of blessings. Though I still hear my state trooper friend's voice every time I enter an expressway, more importantly I hear God's voice, through Scripture: "Yield to [God] and be at peace with Him; thereby good will come to you" (Jb 22:21, NASB).

This idea of yielding to others, either by humbling ourselves to be taught or by putting aside our ambitions in order to serve others, is not one widely promoted today. Most of us are brought up with a "be aggressive and get ahead" mentality. Often, the "American Way" is paved with selfish intent: a desire to live only for yourself, to fulfill your dreams and hopes at whatever the cost, and to satisfy all your personal desires. Pope Francis boldly declares, "Narcissism makes people incapable of looking beyond themselves, beyond their own desires and need."[29] But as Christians we're called to be aware of those around us, and to serve their needs in love.

Yielding to others in service is the more perfect way and yields a great spiritual harvest. How can we respond to this call to serve others in our ordinary daily lives? The very best road map for this is laid out by Jesus in Matthew's Gospel: "For I was hungry and you gave me food, I was thirsty and you gave me drink, I was a stranger and you welcomed me, I was naked and you clothed me, I was sick and you visited me, I was in prison and you came to me" (Mt 25:35–36). These acts that Jesus lists are

WILLIS TOWER
Chicago, Illinois
This is no ordinary office building — take an elevator up 103 floors to experience the highest observation deck in the United States and its Midwestern views.

part of what we call the *corporal works of mercy*. Let's take a line-by-line look at this Scripture passage.

How can we satisfy hunger? "For I was hungry and you gave me food" (Mt 25:35). We can all collect food and donate it, but how about taking it a few steps further? I remember many years ago learning about a family that had a small food budget but still wanted to bless others who were hungry. Instead of buying brand-name products, they decided to buy the store brand. They donated the money they saved to a food pantry. Another family gave up their favorite snacks and cereals once a week and donated them to their parish's St. Vincent de Paul collection. What about asking your mom and dad if your family can clean out your cupboards at least once a month? (Make sure you offer to help!) Your extra nonperishable items could be a blessing to another family.

In addition to giving food to shelters or food banks, you could personally go feed the hungry. Our youth group collected donations for bag lunches. One evening we got together, took time to pray for those in need of food and shelter, and made sandwiches for the homeless in a neighboring city. We put those sandwiches in paper bags with a bottle of water, fruit, cookies, a napkin, and even a toothbrush and toothpaste. We then set out onto the streets (in groups of at least two, and always with an adult) to distribute the lunches. If your youth group hasn't organized such an event, consider speaking to your youth minister about putting one together.

Feeding the hungry doesn't have to be an extraordinary event; it can easily be a regular one, too. You can take small steps toward satisfying hunger. Skip your favorite ice cream spot or after-school fast-food treat, and place that spare change in the poor basket at church. Do something similar during Lent by forgoing all other beverages but water. At the end of the forty days, the money you save can be donated. Keep a small nonperishable food item, such as a granola bar, in your bag or car glove box to give out when encountering someone in need. Consider making dinner to give your mom or dad a night off from cooking. Everyone hungers for Christ, and your witness and actions, through food and hospitality, reflect him. When you satisfy hunger, you are truly yielding to Christ in others.

ROADSIDE DISTRACTIONS

Lucy the Elephant

Margate City, New Jersey

Lucy was built in 1881 by an eccentric Irish Catholic businessman and has been everything from a summer home to a speakeasy, though currently she's simply a tourist attraction.

How do you quench thirst? "I was thirsty and you gave me drink" (Mt 25:35). In the story of the woman at the well, Jesus speaks about not only physical thirst but also spiritual thirst. "Every one who drinks of this water will thirst again, but whoever drinks of the water that I shall give him will never thirst" (Jn 4:13–14). Jesus is the means of quenching that inborn thirst for God's love, which is our deepest thirst. We can feed the hungry and satisfy thirst for knowledge and righteousness through our witness of what God has done in our own life. Social media provides us a new way to share the graces and blessings we have received from God. We do not always need to preach or teach. We merely need to share our testimonies of what God has done for us. In this small way, we can offer the living water to parched souls.

This method of being an example of love can be used when encountering strangers as well. "I was a stranger and you welcomed me" (Mt 25:35). We do not need to go far to find strangers among us. Keep your eyes open in the school hallways, classrooms, and lunchroom for lonely souls. Invite someone who is sitting alone to join you. Give the new kid in school some tips or a quick tour. Include a foreign exchange student in your weekend plans, or consider hosting one. How about peers visiting your parish or youth group? You can begin by welcoming them. Take the time to introduce yourself and to ask if they have any questions about your parish. Smile at your pew neighbors warmly at the sign of peace as you greet them. This is something our Protestant brothers and sisters do so well. We could definitely learn from their example in this area. How often are we reaching out to the visitors at our Masses? As someone who has changed parishes a few times, I know how hard it can be. The kindness of even one person can help a stranger feel connected to a new community, be it at school or church.

Continuing on with Matthew, let's take a look at the beginning of verse thirty-six: "I was naked and you clothed me" (Mt 25:36). How many of us have so many articles of clothing that we have to put away one season's clothes to make room in our drawers and closets for the next one's? How many times have you opened your closet, pulled out a shirt, and thought, "I didn't even know I had this!" Why not go through your clothes (once a season or once a year) and donate what may not fit to a charity or shelter, and really make a choice to bless another person? When we find a two-for-one sale, why not buy two and give one away? If someone doesn't have as much as you, or lacks fashion sense, be kind. Make sure you do not make fun of them. Whenever possible, genuinely compliment them instead.

Clothing the naked doesn't stop with clothes. Those who have lost their hair due to an illness or chemotherapy may also feel naked. If you have long hair (or are willing to grow it out), consider chopping off eight to ten inches and donating it to an organization that will use it to construct a wig for someone in need. May you be open to the many ways you can clothe someone in need, whether through hair, hems, or another generous action.

The next request in the verse at hand can be a bit trickier to fulfill: "I was sick and you visited me" (Mt 25:36). Personally, I am not a big fan of hospitals. I am a serious "germaphobe," so the very idea of walking through the doors of a hospital gives me great anxiety. When my friends are sick, I am not one to cook and bring over a meal either. Honestly, this is partly because I am a lousy cook, so it is probably in their best interest for healing that I don't. Nevertheless, despite our weaknesses, we all have an obligation as Christians to care for the sick. Besides physical care, what are some other options to fulfill this duty? When it comes to caring for the sick, both physically and mentally, we must never underestimate the power of prayer. If you cannot personally care for someone, you should wrap them up in prayer. Meeting the spiritual and physical needs of a person in need, especially someone who is ill, is key to imitating Our Lord. After all, a huge part of Jesus' ministry was healing the infirm.

Another difficult appeal found in Matthew 25:36 is to visit those in prison. Being imprisoned does not refer only to incarceration. There are many people who are not able to leave their home for one reason or another. Things like age, an illness, or even parenting small children can make getting out difficult. Isolation is a tough cross to carry. As a community of Christ, we should look at the needs of all people and discover how we can help them. Can you visit a nursing home for a game night? Can you offer to babysit for someone? Can you pray for an imprisoned soul? It is important to keep our eyes and hearts open to ways of yielding to those in need.

If you don't have the desire to serve others, pray for the grace to do so. As the *Catechism* teaches us, grace is a sharing in the Trinitarian life (CCC 1997). In fact, the very shape of the Yield sign reminds me of the Trinity. The three sides remind me of the Three Persons of the Trinity: God the Father, God the Son, and God the Holy Spirit. Still, it remains one sign just as God remains one God. The Trinity is a perfect union of love. "God is love" (1 Jn 4:8).

We are called to imitate the Trinity, specifically Christ, in our charity toward others. In yielding to others, we have the opportunity to imitate Christ by serving them. Indeed, "the Son of man came not to be served, but to serve" (Mt 20:28). Furthermore, through our charity, we not only imitate Christ, but we also serve him. When we yield to others, we yield to Christ. "Truly, I say to you, as you did it to one of the least of these my brethren, you did to me" (Mt 25:40). Additionally, "the Trinity is a model of Christian family; the Christian family has an evangelizing and missionary task" (CCC 2205). We each have this call to mission and evangelization, and we can fulfill that call by serving others. Your mission field may be far away, but more likely you are being called to serve and witness within your immediate community, perhaps even within the walls of your own home.

HOLY ROAD TRIP

LORETTO CHAPEL

Santa Fe, New Mexico

The gem of this chapel is the unique spiral staircase to the choir loft, built by a mysterious carpenter after the Sisters of Loreto made a novena to St. Joseph.

Yielding to traffic is something we do every day, yet we are not given kudos, a standing ovation, or a certificate for doing so safely. It is just part of being in the community of drivers. Drivers promise to yield to those already on the road and enter onto the road only when it is safe to do so. As a Christian pilgrim, the same standard should apply to the rest of your life. Seek to do unto others as you would have them do unto you (cf. Mt 7:12), put others' concerns before your own, and always be looking out for your neighbor's needs (both physical and spiritual). Pope Francis speaks encouraging words to his flock: "Believing in Jesus means giving him our flesh with the humility and courage of Mary. ... It means giving him our hands, to caress the little ones and the poor; our feet, to go forth and meet our brothers and sisters; our arms, to hold up the weak and to work in the Lord's vineyard; our minds, to think and act in the light of the Gospel; and especially to offer our hearts to love and to make choices in accordance with God's will. All this happens thanks to the working of the Holy Spirit. And in this way we become instruments in God's hands, so that Jesus can act in the world through us."[30]

A friend of mine recently bought a new car. It came with a blind-spot detection feature on the side-view mirror. If someone is traveling alongside her but she can't see them, it alerts her. This is a very handy assistant for merging onto a highway. As I watched the bright yellow-orange arrow blink its alert furiously at her on our recent trip, I couldn't help but imagine what life would be like if we all had a blind-spot alert system to help us recognize fellow travelers. How much better would we be equipped to yield if we could always see those people God has placed with us on this highway to heaven? This new technology might not come ready to be fitted upon our heart, so we have to rely on God to clear up our spiritual blind spots. May our hearts, hands, feet, eyes, and mouth be ready to yield to Christ and others in a spirit of loving service as we take hold of the wheel of life.

QUESTIONS FOR REFLECTION

1. What are the corporal works of mercy, and which one are you most drawn to act upon? How can you serve others in your immediate community?
2. How can the Yield sign remind us of the Trinity?
3. In works of charity, how do we serve Christ? At the same time, how does Jesus work through us (our hands, eyes, mouth, etc.) in acts of service?

SCHOOL CROSSING
MENTORSHIP

Carmen Briceño

He who walks with wise men becomes wise.

PROVERBS 13:20

Perhaps it's because I am a bad driver, or maybe it's because I am impatient, or maybe it's the fact that I am easily distracted (most likely, it is all of the above); whatever the reason, I am always annoyed when encountering School Crossing signs and the mandatory twenty-five-mile-per-hour speed limit. I am roaring ahead, and suddenly I need to slow down to a snail's pace. Trust me, I am not suggesting ignoring those signs; actually, I invite you to explore with me the lessons we can learn from them.

This sign is filled with two silhouettes: a young person being accompanied by an older person. Why doesn't the sign simply depict children walking by themselves across the street? Crossing a busy street by yourself, until you know how to understand and obey traffic signals and be aware of the cars around you, is a dangerous experience. On a deeper level, this duo can prompt us to explore a need that rests in our heart: a desire for mentorship that is a vital part of God's design.

For me, this desire bloomed early in my heart. I am the youngest of three girls, and when I was growing up, my older sisters were everything to me. I wanted to talk, act, and essentially be exactly like them. They were my role models. I watched them as they got ready for dates. I eavesdropped on their conversation with their friends (don't follow my bad example), and I even tried to dress like them. Yet although they loved me, they were not particularly fond of having their kid sister around all the time. At the heart of my actions was a yearning for someone to show me what it truly meant to be "grown up." Since I did not receive it from my family, I slowly turned to other sources: namely my friends and the media. This wasn't a conscious decision. When we lack intentional mentors, we naturally fill the void with whatever is available.

My friends and I would have discussions on relationships, clothing, sports, food, and everything else that affected our life. We, inexperienced as we were, forged our own criteria for what it means to be a man or woman. We further formed our identity with input from other inexperienced teens, and what we gathered from the culture around us. How I wish we had a wise guide of faith accompanying us and leading us through the swarming emotions, hormones, conflicts, and decisions that arose!

If you go to school, you have a teacher. If you practice sports, you have a coach. If you play music, you have an instructor. In other words, when you're learning something important, you always have someone older and more experienced than you training you to do your best. Isn't it strange that when it comes to our purpose in life, to discovering God's design for our lives, and to navigating all the challenges we experience, we think we can simply figure it out on our own? Just like the School Crossing sign, we not only need to slow down, but we also need mentors to guide us safely through these years of peer pressure, media bombardment, hormone attacks, and everything else that is thrown our way.

JELLY BELLY FACTORY
Fairfield, California

You probably never realized that you need to know how jelly beans are made (and we won't even mention the free samples). Factory tours are free and fun.

Have you seen the latest statistics on how much time the average teen spends on watching media per day? According to the Kaiser Family Foundation, the average teen spends an estimated seven and a half hours a day on entertainment media.[31] Now here is the kicker: the average person lives about seventy-seven years. If a person spends seven and a half hours a day on media, over a lifetime that amounts to roughly twenty-one years! If you multitask by texting while watching television, the media consumption increases to roughly ten and a half hours a day. Over a lifetime, that tallies to twenty-eight years!

Let's pretend you wake up one day with complete amnesia. Not only do you not know who you are, but you do not recognize the body you are in or what it is for. A friend, in order to help you out, sits you down and makes you consume seven and a half hours of media a day for a month.

Those 225 hours will include music videos, songs,

television shows, social media, movies, magazines, commercials, and billboards. What image of womanhood or manhood would you receive? At the end of the month, what will you have learned? What if this is all you did for twenty-one years? How would all that media consumption transform you? It's easy for us to think that the media does not affect us, that we can somehow tune it out. Let me tell you, however, that the product, fashion, television, music, movie, food, and diet industries (among others) are paying billions of dollars for advertising because they know full well just how great an impact they actually have on you. The media makes for a poor mentor.

ROADSIDE DISTRACTIONS

Dinosaur Land

White Post, Virginia

Step into the world of the Mesozoic era at this quirky park. It's the perfect photo op — grab a selfie with a velociraptor, or a family portrait with the T-Rex.

Here is another scary statistic. We know that an average teen spends around seven and a half hours a day with media, which amounts to twenty-one years in a lifetime. Did you know that the average Christian spends less than ten minutes a day in prayer, less than seven months in a lifetime? Twenty-one years' worth of media input versus seven months of God's input in a lifetime! With these statistics, God's design for you does not stand a chance against the media's bombardment.

Now let's imagine the same scenario as before, where you wake up one day with complete amnesia. Instead of a friend putting a computer and a phone in front of you, a different friend begins to tell you about God. At her encouragement, you begin to read the Bible and the lives of the saints, to serve the poor, to participate in the Sacraments, to imitate Christ, and to spend time with other friends who are also turning to God for their identity. After all this time, what will you have learned about what it means to be a man or woman and what your purpose is? Would you be different from when you had the media as your mentor?

As a teenager, in that awkward stage between childhood and adulthood, you're learning how to navigate new roads. Because you haven't crossed them before, it's vital to have someone with you who can help you avoid the dead ends and stay safely on the narrow road. When my friends and I were teenagers, having a mentor would have freed us from many heartaches and mistakes. It is also God's wisdom and plan for us: "He who walks with wise men becomes wise" (Prv 13:20). Look and pray for women or men you can look up to and trust to be good mentors. A good mentor is someone who will challenge you to greatness, who will hold you accountable to truth and virtue, and who will show you by their own example how to live. A really good mentor will be able to help you hold up a mirror to yourself and show you in what areas you need to grow and develop.

Don't forget, you can be a woman or man younger girls or boys can look up to. You may have younger siblings, or maybe your friends do — have you noticed how they'll try to imitate you or be in the same room with you and your friends? Just like you desire mentorship, so do those around you. Look to make a gift of yourself by being a guide to those who are younger than you.

Do you want to be unique and original? Then your goal should be to become whom God created you to be! God has a personal, individual, tailored plan for you.

God doesn't treat us like Hollywood does. If you can't accomplish the mission he has envisioned for your happiness, he won't cast someone else in your role. I clearly remember when a priest friend of mine noticed my spiritual discouragement and reminded me that saints are not reincarnated. I was never meant to be Mother Teresa 2.0. He calls each of us simply to be the best version of ourselves. Pope Francis said it best in his Apostolic Exhortation *Gaudete et Exultate*: "We should not grow discouraged before examples of holiness that appear unattainable. There are some testimonies that may prove helpful and inspiring, but that we are not meant to copy, for that could even lead us astray from the one specific path that the Lord has in mind for us. The important thing is that each believer discern his or her own path, that they bring out the very best of themselves, the most personal gifts that God has placed in their hearts (cf. 1 Cor 12:7), rather than hopelessly trying to imitate something not meant for them."[32] That is why mentorship is so important. A mentor, by his or her example and support, can help you discover this unique mission God has given you.

As you cross the road of life, are you walking alone? God desires community for you in friendship and mentors. Where can you seek a mentor? These relationships can naturally form by attending a youth group or similar community. You may find the youth minister or adult leaders inspiring or helpful. Other mentors could include priests, a friend's mom or dad, an aunt or uncle, coach, teacher, or college student. When you are confirmed, you select a Confirmation sponsor. Choose one based on his or her good example and wisdom. After the sacrament, do not lose touch with this person. Instead, continue to build a relationship with your sponsor. Keep them up to date on what you are involved in, and how you are growing in your faith. Above all, share your desire with God to be authentically mentored. He will direct your path.

We also have great examples in the saints, who can truly be our friends and guides through heartfelt prayer. Saint Catherine of Siena was an amazing woman of prayer, and had a great role to play in the politics of her time. Saint Joan of Arc led an army in the name of Christ. Saint Teresa of Avila reformed the Carmelite order, and Saint Faustina had visions of Jesus and was given the incredible message of Divine Mercy. Saint Gianna Beretta Mola gave her life for her child. Blessed Chiara Badano lived a beautiful life as a teen and died at eighteen from cancer, with a smile on her face, and changed the lives of millions. Blessed Pier Giorgio Frassati was an athlete, mountain climber, pool player, and all-around attractive, joyful man. He used his youth and great wealth to help the poor in secret. Isidore Bakanja stood up for his faith and preferred death rather than yield to the pressure of removing his scapular and Rosary at his work site. Venerable Matt Talbot converted from his drunken ways, and Saint Augustine left behind a life of promiscuity and sexual sin.

HOLY ROAD TRIP

SHRINE OF OUR LADY OF MARTYRS
Auriesville, New York

Located in what was formerly the Mohawk village of Ossernenon, the shrine church marks where North American Martyrs Saints Isaac Jogues, René Goupil, and John Lalande were martyred.

Mentorship from wise earthly and heavenly guides helps shape us in the good and beautiful life. These guides are meant to inspire us to a life of virtue (good habits), and see that people are still living for God, and that it is indeed possible! We need to practice small virtues that will make us become who we were created to be. Don't become a bad imitation of someone else; become the full-blown version of who God created you to be!

Foster good relationships with other women and men who want to live an authentic life. We all need companions on the journey! It is much easier to stay on the right track when we have people traveling with us that share the same vision. Sports are won as a team, and wars are defeated by an army. Don't try to do it alone.

Pray and get to know the God who created you. Get to know his design for your life, and his vision for womanhood or manhood. Don't be like the average Christian who gives God less than ten minutes a day while giving the media seven and a half hours. Yield to God by giving him a real voice in your life. Don't settle for what others say about God, but personally turn to him. Take time to read his words and listen to his voice. Relationships are personal and cannot be delegated. Take one last look at our road sign. Notice the two figures in the picture? I hope that every time you see the School Crossing sign it reminds you that you are not alone. In your journey, God is walking with you through other holy men and women, through Mary and the saints, and by his Holy Spirit. You only need to reach out your hand.

QUESTIONS FOR REFLECTION

1. How does the media often substitute for authentic mentorship? How do you think your media consumption affects you in this area?
2. How can you be the best version of yourself? How are you personally called to sainthood, uniquely?
3. As you cross the road of life, are you walking alone? What is the importance of mentorship? Where can you seek a mentor here on earth, and in heaven?
4. Is there a particular saint you feel drawn to that you think could help you in your current stage of life and in your challenges?

DEER CROSSING
FAITH AND SCIENCE

Jennessa Terraccino

Ever since the creation of the world his invisible nature, namely, his eternal power and deity, has been clearly perceived in the things that have been made.

ROMANS 1:20

One early morning, I woke up to a lot of commotion in my house. My oldest brother and his borrowed car had a surprise attack from nature. He returned home quite shaken up, and recalled the story of a startling bash while driving down the road. Quickly he pulled over the car to investigate, but he saw no sign of any animal, so he concluded it must have been a bird. After hearing the details of the wreck, the skeptic in me thought something didn't sound right. I went out to examine the car on my own. The dent was huge, so my first thought was that it must have been one really big bird. But then I noticed deer hair in all the crevices. Upon further investigation by my father, it turns out the deer hit the car in a kind of leap and run. In an attempt to bound over the road, it found my brother's car in the way, but somehow managed to continue for a short while. The evidence lay on the other side of the road. Thankfully, my brother was safe.

Sightings of Deer Crossing signs followed by actual deer are common in the Virginia suburb in which I dwelled. I never forgot what happened to my brother, so I was always extra cautious on the road, especially at night. I'd do an old-lady hunch and hold my steering wheel really tight during the twilight hours. My eyes would dart back and forth across my path looking for the glimmer of animal eyes catching my headlights. If I saw a deer, I would slow to a crawl and my body would stiffen.

Nature can be intimidating, but it can also be revealing. As Christians, we are called to live by faith and to follow the precepts of the Holy Catholic Church. With that in mind, does the natural world have a place in our faith? Are we allowed to be skeptics? Is it okay to use science to investigate and question faith? Or do we need to dodge science, as we do deer, when it comes to faith in Christ?

Before we dive into those questions, it is important to set a foundation. Saint John Paul II in his encyclical letter *Fides et Ratio* (Faith and Reason) reminds us that approaching truth takes both our heart and our head. "Faith and reason are like two wings on which the human spirit rises to the contemplation of truth."[33] God gave us an intellect and the ability to reason, but he also desires our faith. Remember that Jesus tells Thomas, who did not believe in the resurrected Christ without tangible evidence and touch, "Blessed are those who have not seen and yet believe" (Jn 20:29).

We cannot put our complete faith in science and turn skeptic to anything lacking physical proof; but as Christians, we can certainly see the usefulness of science in aiding our faith and our understanding of truth. After all, Jesus allowed Thomas the gift of that physical evidence when he invited the doubting Apostle to touch his resurrected body and wounds (Jn 20:27). Nevertheless, Saint John Paul II warns us not to make science an idol,[34] and so does Scripture: "Therefore God gave

PIT STOP

SMITHSONIAN NATIONAL ZOO
Washington, DC.

One among many free Smithsonian museums in Washington, DC, this massive zoo holds around three hundred species of animals. Don't miss the giant pandas!

them up ... because they exchanged the truth about God for a lie and worshipped and served the creature rather than the creator" (Rom 1:24–25). Christians and scientists are united in their thirst for truth, and it is precisely that yearning that has us both searching for answers.[35]

Today there often exists a falsely attributed idea that the Church is opposed to science. But a second look at history might surprise you. As it turns out, the Church had a friendly relationship with many scientists, and many priests and religious made some very significant contributions to science. For instance, Polish astronomer Nicholas Copernicus was consulted by the Vatican on multiple occasions, and one of his books was even dedicated to Pope Paul III.[36] Father Clauvis was a mathematician who created the Gregorian calendar, which replaced the problematic old Julian calendar.[37] Father Stanley Jaki, a prizewinning historian of science, was a key player in establishing laws of motion. Saint Albert the Great (Albertus Magnus), who stressed the importance of direct observation, was named the patron of all who "cultivate the natural sciences."[38] Father Nicolaus Steno is known for his theory of fossils, that rocks can reveal the world's past.[39]

Perhaps most significant are the discoveries of the Jesuits (the Society of Jesus), an order of priests that still exists today (Pope Francis is one). Throughout history, this group of priests contributed many scientific breakthroughs, such as pendulum clocks, barometers, reflecting telescopes, and microscopes. They produced theories of blood circulation, flight, and connections between the moon and tides. Furthermore, they created star maps, helped with flood control, invented plus and minus signs in Italian mathematics, learned meteorology, and made improvements in seismology. They also took on the task of recording all their findings in massive encyclopedia.[40] They spread their knowledge throughout the world to China, India, Africa, and Central and South America.[41] The list of their discoveries continues!

With all that in mind, what does the natural world that scientists find so fascinating reveal to us about God? Saint Thomas Aquinas, a Doctor of the Church, taught that you could come to know God through creation if you took the time to think through the logic. The *Catechism of the Catholic Church* states, "By natural reason, man can know God with certainty, on the basis of his works" (CCC 50). Saint Paul tells us in the Bible that we are without excuse in coming to know God because "ever since the creation of the world his invisible nature, namely, his eternal power and deity, has been clearly perceived in the things that have been made" (Rom 1:20). Unlike my response to Deer Crossing signs, the Church isn't afraid of facing the natural world. Saint

John Paul II states: "Faith therefore has no fear of reason, but seeks it out and has trust in it. Just as grace builds on nature and brings it to fulfillment, so faith builds upon and perfects reason."[42] If someone has never heard the Gospel, that person could still come to know that there is a God. (Without divine revelation, however, you could not know truths such as that Jesus is the Savior of the world, or that God is a Trinity of persons.) Saint Thomas outlines these natural means in his *Summa Theologiae*. They are known as the five ways, or proofs, of God's existence.

The first argument is the **unmoved mover**; this way considers motion in the world. "Where there is motion, there is a mover, and ultimately a first mover."[43] Just as if a car is moving, there must be a driver (or at least an engineer). The second is the **first cause**, which can remind us of that funny question, "Which came first, the chicken or the egg?" In the world, "there must be a first cause which is itself uncaused. This is God."[44] The third is an argument about **contingency**, things that don't have to exist. Deer are contingent. Life would go on with or without them. Behind contingent things is a necessary being, which is God.[45] The fourth way considers "the scale of **perfection** in the world."[46] The natural world, like cars, has a wide scope. Some cars are fancier, faster, and more expensive than others. Some deer have larger antlers, are stronger, and are faster than others. In the world things are more or less good, better, and still better. "Where there are degrees of perfection, there must ultimately be absolute perfection. This is God."[47] The fifth and final way is from final causes or ends. Cars are designed by humans to work in a certain way. A car starts, goes, and stops. Creatures are designed to work in a certain way too. Deer eat, grow, run, and multiply. A deer can never grow into a duck, because a deer has a certain nature. This logic points us to a first designer and first governor.[48] If you would find it absurd for a car to fall out of the sky perfectly designed, how much more absurd the myriad of different DNA in thousands of creatures in the world? Design comes from a designer. (If you want to know more, there are some great books entirely on Aquinas's proofs.)

ROADSIDE DISTRACTIONS

Lenny the Chocolate Moose

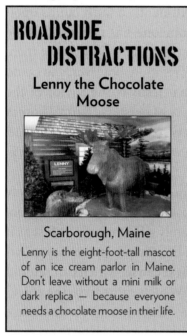

Scarborough, Maine

Lenny is the eight-foot-tall mascot of an ice cream parlor in Maine. Don't leave without a mini milk or dark replica — because everyone needs a chocolate moose in their life.

The natural and supernatural are not enemies. In fact, many times the Church has turned to science about miraculous encounters. This is precisely because "Catholicism admits the possibility of miracles and acknowledges the role of the supernatural, but the very idea of a miracle suggests that the event in question is *unusual*, and of course it is only against the backdrop of an orderly natural world that a miracle can be recognized in the first place."[49] Throughout Scripture we see countless miracles: bones healing (cf. 2 Kgs 13:21), heavenly bread provided (cf. 1 Kgs 17:16; Ex 16:1–15; Mt 14:13–21), lions suddenly tamed (cf. Dn 6:20), water being turned into wine (cf. Jn 2:1–11), a dead man coming out of his tomb (cf. Jn 11:43–44), blind men recovering their sight (cf. Mt 9:27–30), appearances of angels (cf. Jn 20:11–12), Jesus' resurrection (cf. Lk 24), and so much more. Such miraculous encounters did not end when the last letter of Scripture was penned. Today, amazing phenomena still occur, such as apparitions of Our Lady or the Eucharist turning to physical flesh, and oftentimes science helps verify their miraculous nature.

The Blessed Virgin Mother has supernaturally appeared throughout history in different cultures, under an array of titles, bringing important messages to one or more persons at a time. Marian apparitions are considered private revelation, and the faithful are not bound to accept them, but when the Church confirms an apparition, she declares that it is worthy of belief. Private revelations reconfirm a known aspect of public revelation, but do not add anything new to the deposit of faith. When a purported apparition takes place, the Church has a process of approval to explore whether it truly did take place.

The process begins with the local diocesan bishop. At the request of that bishop, the national conference of bishops may intervene or the Apostolic See. Next, the apparition is investigated using the following positive criteria: First, the event must be morally certain (that is, it undoubtedly occurred). Second, the person who claimed to see Our Lady must be evaluated for things like mental balance, honesty, a strong moral life, and obedience to the Church. Third, the content of the message must be reviewed to make sure it does not conflict with the Church's teaching on faith and morals. Finally, the revelation should encourage healthy devotions and positive spiritual fruits in people's lives through prayer, conversion, and works of charity.[50]

Negative criteria are also used to validate the apparition. There cannot be evidence of errors regarding the facts of what took place. The apparition cannot have any doctrinal errors. The Church makes sure there is no evidence of financial gain related to the promotion of the apparition. Finally, the person claiming to have seen the apparition must be free of any grave immoral acts and any psychological disorders (this requires help from psychological sciences).[51]

My favorite Marian apparition is Our Lady of Guadalupe, and the tilma that remains hundreds of years later. The story begins in the year 1531. At that time, pagan Aztecs, who believed their gods demanded human sacrifice, ruled Mexico. Under their rule, a humble man named Juan Diego remained a faithful Catholic. As he walked his normal route to Mass through Tepeyac Hill (modern Mexico City), he heard music and a voice calling out to him by name. He saw a vision of a beautiful lady who said she was the perpetual Virgin Mary. She requested that a church be built in her honor at the site, and that he go to Bishop Zumarraga to make this request.

After two visits, the bishop requested a sign from Juan Diego to validate the story. On December 12, Mary appeared to Juan Diego and told him to gather flowers from the barren, cactus-filled Tepeyac Hill. In the middle of winter, he found roses of a type not native to Mexico. He gathered them and brought them to Our Lady. She placed the flowers in his tilma (a cactus-fiber smock-like garment) and sent him to seek out the bishop. Once before Bishop Zumarraga, Juan Diego opened his tilma to show the bishop the bouquet. After the roses fell, an image of Our Lady of Guadalupe was visible on the tilma. The bishop believed, and so did nine million Aztec Indians, who converted to Catholicism.[52]

Nearly five hundred years later, we can still look upon the same tilma in the Basilica of Our Lady of Guadalupe in Mexico City. Made primarily out of cactus fibers, which typically last only up to thirty years, the tilma has miraculously survived hundreds of years and a bombing by twenty-nine sticks of dynamite. In 1979, Dr. Philip Serna Callahan, a biophysicist and an expert in infrared photography, studied the fabric. After his investigation, he could offer no scientific explanation for the image, and discovered that the tilma maintains a constant temperature of 98.6 Fahrenheit, the same as the body of a living person.[53] Another doctor, Carlos Fernandez del Castillo, placed a stethoscope below the black band at the waist of Our Lady (the Aztec's symbol of pregnancy) and heard rhythmic repeating heartbeats at 115 beats per minute, the same as that of a baby in the maternal womb.[54] In 1981, Dr. Juan Hernández Illescas did an astronomical study of the stars that adorn the mantle of Our Lady. He discovered an accurate constellation map which astronomers believe shows the very stars in the sky the day of the apparition: December 12, 1531. A Peruvian ophthalmologist, Dr. José Aste Tonsmann, an expert in digital processing of images, digitally enlarged the image of Our Lady's eyes by 2,500 times their actual size under extremely high resolution. Within her eyes, he found reflections of two scenes containing thirteen persons, including Bishop Zumarraga and the other witnesses when they first saw the image.[55]

Physical evidence of another miracle, even older than the tilma, remains. In Lanciano, Italy, a Eucharistic miracle occurred in the year 700. A priest-monk was celebrating Mass and "suffered from recurrent doubts regarding transubstantiation (the change of the bread and wine into the Body and Blood of Christ). He had just spoken the solemn words of Consecration when the Host was suddenly changed into a circle of flesh, and the wine was transformed into visible blood."[56] The miraculous Host and five pellets of coagulated blood were placed in a special vessel called a reliquary, made of ivory and passed through the safekeeping of three different religious orders. Today, it is kept in a silver and crystal monstrance and chalice in Italy.

Over the span of hundreds of years the miracle of Lanciano has been verified again and again. Most recently, in 1970, it was studied by Dr. Odoardo Linoli, a professor and expert in anatomy, chemistry, and clinical microscopy. A small sample was removed from one of the blood pellets, and the Host turned to flesh, in order to scientifically examine both. Upon investigation, the flesh was found to be a "striated muscular tissue of the myocardium (heart wall) … both the flesh and sample of blood were found to be of human origin … the blood and the flesh were found to belong to the same blood type, AB."[57] Furthermore, it was noted that if the blood had been removed from a cadaver, it would have "altered rapidly through spoilage and decay,"[58] yet 1,300 years later it remains unspoiled. No preservatives were detected in the examination. Finally, the particular heart tissue that was identified would be very difficult to acquire through anatomic dissection.

More recently, a Eucharistic miracle took place in 1996, on the feast of the Assumption, this time in Buenos Aires, Argentina. After a Mass was celebrated in the parish of Santa Maria y Caballito Almagro, a woman approached Father Alejandro Pezet because she believed she had come across a desecrated Host on a candlestick in the back of the church. When the priest sought to dispose of the Host in a glass of water, according to canon law, instead of the Host dissolving, it appeared to become a bloody piece of flesh. A few weeks later, the miraculous Host was photographed.[59]

After three years, the Host, which was stored in a tabernacle, showed no sign of decay. Pope Francis — Bishop Bergoglio at that time — opened a formal investigation. A sample of the blood was then sent for forensic analysis to San Francisco. In order not to influence the scientists, they were not informed about how the sample originated. The test results revealed that it was human blood, type AB+. The investigation continued with Dr. Frederick Zugibe of Columbia University in New York, a distinguished cardiologist and forensic pathologist. He "testified that it was 'a fragment of the heart muscle found in the wall of the left ventricle close to the valves.' Because white blood cells had

HOLY ROAD TRIP

THE BLACK MADONNA SHRINE
Eureka, Missouri

Nestled in the foothills of the Ozarks, the little shrine to Our Lady of Czestochowa was built by a Polish Franciscan, who also constructed several grottoes around the monastery gardens.

penetrated the tissue, he stated that 'the heart had been under severe stress, as if the owner had been beaten severely about the chest.' "[60]

Next, the lab reports were compared with the data collected from the Eucharistic miracle of Lanciano, Italy. Again, the sample's origins were not shared with the scientists. The results are astounding! They reported that the two samples must be the same. "Both samples revealed an 'AB'-positive blood type, which occurs in 5% of the population. The DNA is identical, and there are features to indicate that the man came from the Middle

East."[61] The miracles of Lanciano and Buenos Aires are just two of the 140 Vatican-approved Eucharistic miracles.

As you journey through life, many people will seek to challenge your faith or your understanding of it. When those times come, make sure you aren't a deer in the headlights! As a Christian, questioning your faith and searching for answers is not a problem. It is precisely these moments that will bring you to deeper faith and knowledge. The Church offers you a font of miracles, writings, teachings, lives of the saints, and more. If you have a specific question, chances are a pope, saint, theologian, or a scientist already attempted to provide an answer.

If you are looking to go deeper in faith and science, you can consider the following: over seventy thousand people saw the miracle of the sun (related to a Marian apparition) in Fatima, Portugal in 1917; several saints' bodies have never known the normal process of decay after death (they are known as incorrupt); and the Shroud of Turin very well may be the burial cloth of Christ, and has many scientifically intriguing qualities.

Next time you see a Deer Crossing sign, as you slow down to proceed cautiously, consider taking the time for quick contemplation of God in creation. On the road of life, keep your eyes open wide with faith, or nature might misdirect you or tempt you to make it something more than it is. Creation is vast and beautiful, and evidence for the Creator that all our hearts and minds seek. "All creatures of our God and King, / Lift up your voice and with us sing. / O praise Him! Alleluia!"[62]

QUESTIONS FOR REFLECTION

1. How do faith and reason work together?
2. What is the Church's attitude toward science? Are you surprised by the amount of contributions by Catholics to the field of science? Why or why not?
3. According to Saint Thomas, and your own observations, how can the natural world reveal God? How can creation lead us toward God the creator, not away from him?
4. What miracle described in this chapter fascinated you most? Why? Are you surprised by the process of verification that the Church goes through?

MERGE
DATING DOS AND DON'TS
Keeley Bowler

It is not good that the man should be alone.

GENESIS 2:18

Y ou can't drive on a single-lane road forever. There comes a time when you have to merge onto a highway, where you can travel faster and more efficiently. Usually this requires cranking your neck quite a bit and hitting the gas as you merge! The purpose of the Merge sign is to help you safely and effectively join the highway traffic. Moving from a single-lane to a multi-lane highway can remind us of our desire to be close to others on our journey to heaven. We move from a single lane (solitude) to a larger road with double lanes (communion with others; be it friendship, romantic love, or marriage).

We all desire communion with others. Most of our actions are motivated by a desire to be closer to others, whether it is our family, friends, or that cute guy or girl in our English class. A verse in Genesis speaks to the desire written on our hearts: "It is not good for the man to be alone" (Gn 2:18). God created in us a desire for community with others. On the flip side, we also see that love — both friendship and romantic love — can cause pain. Around us we see the consequences of love gone wrong: divorces that split families apart, sexually transmitted infections, unwanted pregnancies, depression, loneliness, bullying, and betrayal. Sometimes the world can seem like nothing more than a highway of broken hearts. It makes us wonder — is this desire to be close to others a good thing? Is there a way to love that doesn't risk our mind, bodies, and soul?

Let's consider the Merge sign some more. When you are driving and you see this sign, it reminds you to be aware of your surroundings and enter cautiously. Highway travel is worth the risk and provides more advantages than navigating the single-lane back roads. In the same way, seeking closeness with others is worth the risk as long as you learn the rules of the road and proceed cautiously. If love and friendship are worthy endeavors, even holy ones, then how can you navigate fulfilling these desires without falling into the common pitfalls you see peers, family members, and celebrities succumbing to in their lives?

Many of the most important clues we have regarding rules for interacting with others are found in our bodies. We can look at our body and understand why God created us and how he wants us to live. Just as roadways have a discernable design and order, our bodies also contain inherent relational truths that can be uncovered by close observation, and even science.

Imagine if that were part of an ancient civilization from thousands of years ago that was recently discovered. Experts would be able to deduce quite a lot about the civilization just by studying the layout of the city and its structures. Similarly, if an alien landed on earth right now, knowing nothing, he could probably understand the direction of the roadways and infer the meaning of the road signs merely by observing traffic patterns. There is an order, a design, present in roadways that indicates their purpose and the intention of the designers. Notably, if he managed to find himself behind the wheel of a car, our alien would soon learn that the configuration of roads implies a right way to drive and a reckless way.

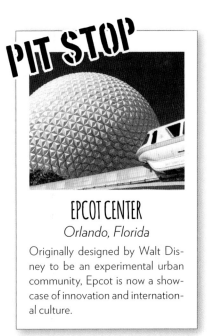

EPCOT CENTER
Orlando, Florida

Originally designed by Walt Disney to be an experimental urban community, Epcot is now a showcase of innovation and international culture.

In the same way, we can come to know certain truths about how we are meant to interact with others merely by studying our bodies. The bodies of a man and woman are complementary, and designed for union. When they join together as the "one flesh" described in the Bible (Gn 2:24; cf. Mt 19:5–6), there is harmony. Simply put, they fit. This physical truth reflects God's desire for earthly marriage: man and woman are called to be a gift to one another.[63] This union is both figuratively and literally fruitful, lending itself to a blossoming of happiness and goodwill as well as to the literal fruitfulness of the resulting child.

God, in sculpting our anatomy, has given each gender a role proper to the exchange of love. The man's role in procreation is to initiate the gift; the woman receives and nurtures the gift, concretely so in the form of pregnancy and motherhood.[64] These respective roles often (and appropriately) play out in dating. Men and women are most able to enjoy the courting process when the man takes on the role of initiator, risking rejection, and the woman can choose whether or not to say yes to his advances. Although the "putting it all on the line" and "waiting patiently to be pursued" postures both have pros and cons, there is a romance to the traditional interaction between the genders that cannot be reproduced by the modern narrative that men and women are interchangeable. The roles, though different, are equal in importance and are both absolutely necessary.

ROADSIDE DISTRACTIONS

World's Largest Man-Made Turtle

Dunseith, North Dakota

Two thousand steel wheel rims and a little imagination gets you things like this giant turtle, which exists solely for your road trip amusement.

What about monogamy, the union of one man and one woman? Can we similarly find the evidence for this truth by examining our bodies? Throughout history, the Catholic Church has taught that sex is meant to be between one man and one woman within the context of the Sacrament of Matrimony. This isn't an arbitrary rule; it's how God designed us. It is the best and safest route to relational happiness. Modern neuroscience backs this up beautifully with its recent focus on understanding the hormonal pathways associated with sexual activity and how they foster a sense of relational closeness and love. Especially in women, there is one principal hormonal actor, oxytocin, which is responsible for conferring many of the changes in the brain that are associated with bonding, sexual activity, and love.[65] (It is worth noting that although oxytocin is the principal actor in women, there is also a similar mechanism in men, though the exact hormones and the physiological response to one's partner differ somewhat.)[66]

Oxytocin works by altering the pleasure center of the brain to release dopamine, the chemical responsible for happy feelings, whenever one is in the presence of the loved one.[67] This is the same mechanism of the brain that is responsible for the high that cocaine users experience.[68] It is easy to see why romantic love, especially its early stages, is so addictive and enjoyable. Oxytocin is such an elemental aspect of bonding that it is released at peak amounts in a woman during sex to establish a bond with her husband, and also during birth and breastfeeding to establish a bond between mother and baby.[69]

Oxytocin has another effect besides creating feelings of euphoria: it is also responsible for increasing feelings of trust and inhibiting reservations.[70] To further solidify this theory, one study administered intranasal oxytocin to half of the test subjects and had them speak with a researcher posing as a financial advisor. The study found that the subjects primed with oxytocin gave the financial advisor twice as much money as did the control group.[71] This study illustrates that oxytocin can effectively shut down the part of our brains responsible for skepticism, making us more trusting and more vulnerable to others.

As mentioned, oxytocin is released at peak amounts during sex, but it is also released to a lesser extent whenever a woman is sexually aroused.[72] That means long hours making out on the couch can begin to initiate the bonding mechanisms in the pleasure center of our brains. Even a twenty-second hug can trigger a small burst of oxytocin.[73] The longer the duration of the relationship and the amount of time the couple spends in physical involvement, the deeper the bond.[74] The smell or even the sight of one's beloved can trigger releases of oxytocin, reinforcing the bond over and over again with happy feelings.[75]

Within the context of marriage, the action of oxytocin and other bonding hormones is beneficial. It encourages feelings of trustworthiness and well-being between partners. It supports marital fidelity.[76] Moreover, the bond between two lovers has calming effects on the experience of pain or distressing situations. One study demonstrated that test subjects registered a muted response to pain on brain scans when holding their partner's hand.[77] Love is a powerful force! Thanks to modern advances in neurobiology, scientists can literally see how the brain correlates to the heart.

Clearly, man was not made to drive in solitude, but merging our life with another's should be done with care and consideration. Merging onto a highway is one of the hardest tasks to accomplish in driving. It involves a keen sensitivity to timing and an awareness of other drivers. If you recklessly merge without regard to the other cars, or weave between multiple lanes because you can't settle on just one, you'll cause a serious accident. Also, if you have bad timing, or drive too fast, you could get seriously hurt. When we merge into a relationship without regard for consequences, what happens? When a person starts to trigger the hormonal bonding pathway with someone who is not his or her spouse, this situation is far from ideal. When that bond is broken in the case of a breakup, the results can be devastating. The experience is not unlike an addict going through withdrawal. There is an increase in stress hormones.[78] Activity in the amygdala, the center of the brain responsible for emotions, triggers fear. Many of the same areas of the brain that are important for conferring physical pain and grief are activated.[79] Men and women are both susceptible to depression following the breakup of a relationship. The stress may be processed differently depending on gender: women are more susceptible to stress-related diseases and men more inclined to substance abuse.[80]

Teenagers are especially vulnerable to increased risk of mental-health disorders following a sexual relationship. It was found that sexually active teenage girls were three times more likely to be depressed than peers who were abstinent, and boys twice as likely. The rates of suicide are dramatically increased among sexually active teens — especially boys, whose rate increases sevenfold.[81] Not to mention that about one in four sexually active teens will contract sexually transmitted infections (STIs),[82] which furthers the likelihood that they will become depressed.[83] Not respecting God's "rules of the road" in regard to merging with others can have painful and lasting consequences. No exceptions apply.

If loving another person means doing what is best for him or her, is it love to become physically involved before marriage? How should you treat the person you have a crush on or are in a relationship with? Is it loving to make him or her vulnerable to depression, an STI, or an unwanted pregnancy? Your road trip to heaven is much smoother when you acknowledge God's truth evident in your body and brain: sexual activity is best reserved for that one person you can count on to be faithful to you for life, who loves you for who you are and not just for the pleasure your body can bring — the person who chooses you as the mother or father of their children.

This means that when you are not yet committed in marriage, there are some physical guidelines to consider. Avoid kissing for extended periods of time. It leads to arousal and begins to trigger the bonding process in our brains that is best left for marriage. Not to mention that it can become difficult to stop at kissing. Before you even start cuddling and light kissing, it is best to get to know whether someone is really worthy of your trust. Remember the experiment with the financial advisor? Oxytocin starts to kick in and inhibit one's ability to discern whether this is the right relationship. We all know guys or girls who are in relationships that are not good for them but they don't have the willpower to break it off. Much of the reason for this blindness is that the physical activity has clouded their judgment to the extent that they are too attached to let go.

Besides the hormonal bonding pathway and the resulting vulnerability to mental health disorders, there are other concerns made plain by science and medicine that should also make you wary about premature physical involvement. The so-called "safe sex" promoted by the media and sex education groups is not actually safe. The failure rate of condoms is high, especially among teenagers, due to breaking, slipping, or misuse.[84] Many of the common STIs can be contracted from oral sex[85] or despite condom use.[86] Even skin-to-skin rubbing from genital contact can be enough to contract human papillomavirus (HPV).[87] Not only does contraception not adequately protect against STIs, but it is also far from foolproof for protecting against unwanted pregnancies. In fact, one study found that 50 percent of women seeking abortion were using contraception at the time of conception.[88]

Common sense confirms that saving sex for marriage is not some outdated religious dictum. It is a truth written plainly in our bodies, and can be understood through science. God created us for love. One of the most fulfilling ways of experiencing that love is through the marital act, a sign of God's love that brings us closer to our spouses and allows for the creation of new life. This is a much more compelling and romantic reality than anything the media tell us.

After you grasp and internalize the fundamental truths of chastity, the next step is to explore its practical implications in the context of dating. The purpose of dates should not be to seek sexual pleasure from the other, but to get to know him or her as a friend. This may require not spending a ton of time alone together. When you are alone, it can be difficult to resist the temptation to express your affection physically. The discipline required here serves not only to honor the dignity of the other but to allow you to grow in the virtue of temperance, which is immeasurably useful in marriage and life in general.

The reason for this discipline is that there is no way of really knowing if this is your future spouse until you meet at the altar. The person may be someone else's future spouse, and you want to ensure you deliver him or her to their spouse unscathed. Consider applying the Golden Rule — "whatever you wish that men would do to you, do so to them" (Mt 7:12) — in dating. Your future spouse may be dating someone else currently. What would you hope they were doing or not doing? Relationships, even engagements, can break up. In the moment, you may feel like you are in love and destined to marry, but true love requires more than these strong feelings. Feelings rarely last. Lasting love requires commitment that remains steadfast despite the near-constant fluctuations of loving, euphoric feelings. Given the seriousness of sex and the possibility of children, the only appropriate level of commitment for sex is lifelong marriage and not simply being "in love."

If you are a teenager, it may be years before you will be married. You may not meet the right person until well after college. It is important that, in the meantime, you navigate romantic interests cautiously, perhaps even waiting until later in life to begin dating. The purpose of dating is to decide if this is the person God is calling you to marry. It is not, as is often practiced, to get emotionally and physically close to someone without the spiritual protection provided by the Sacrament of Matrimony. Commonly, a boyfriend and girlfriend for whom you felt so strongly will be nothing more than a distant memory or regret ten years from now. Dating without premature intimacy is a much better way to make a decision about whether or not he or she has the character required to withstand the many challenges presented in marriage. You are able to consider him or her from a more practical, detached perspective when strong hormonal forces are not obscuring your judgment.

Even if you do not feel currently ready to date (either you are not ready to seriously consider marriage, or there is no one in your vicinity who is virtuous and to whom you are attracted), you can still use this time to proactively prepare for a married or celibate vocation. One way to make a period of prolonged singleness fruitful is to pray intentionally for your future spouse. Your spouse needs the spiritual support! Also, in doing so, you begin to make him or her a priority in your life. It is wise to keep your future spouse in the forefront of your mind as you make important decisions in relationships that will have lasting consequences for your marriage. You can practice being faithful to your spouse even before you meet him or her! This well-earned faithfulness before marriage will be a great gift to give your spouse someday, and an indicator of your trustworthiness.

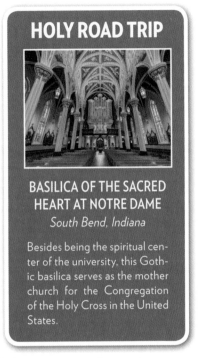

HOLY ROAD TRIP

BASILICA OF THE SACRED HEART AT NOTRE DAME
South Bend, Indiana

Besides being the spiritual center of the university, this Gothic basilica serves as the mother church for the Congregation of the Holy Cross in the United States.

Also, while you are single, it is important to build a good support network. As mentioned before, God wants us to have deep, meaningful relationships. They are essential components of our earthly happiness. Friendship with like-minded peers, family members, and mentors (see "School Crossing: Mentorship") allows us to share happy memories, receive good counsel, and experience God's love.

Mentors can help us navigate the tricky process of

merging — that is, finding a spouse. For one, they can provide needed perspective about whether or not a romantic partner is the right choice. (This assumes your friends share your relationship goals and faith convictions.) These types of godly companions can hold you accountable on the ways you need to improve, including breaking up with that boyfriend or girlfriend who is not marriage material. Parents in particular can be excellent partners in helping you discern relationships, because they love and know you so well.

Selfless love as described in this chapter is not easy. It requires supernatural graces from the perfect model and selfless lover, Jesus on the cross. God wants to give you those graces to love perfectly like he does. You must stay close to him and constantly seek his help through prayer, the sacraments, and frequent reception of the Eucharist. God created marriage and romantic love as an icon of his love for us. It is no surprise that the Devil tries to destroy this captivating icon, and in doing so creates doubt and division among God's children. If we go to God, he can make us heroes and prophets who can return true love to its proper place. The Holy Spirit can guide you to a safe and successful "merge" so you can enjoy the relationships and marriage that he will delight in giving you.

QUESTIONS FOR REFLECTION

1. What is the purpose of oxytocin, and how does it affect a person and impact relationships? How does science support the Church's teaching on waiting until marriage to be physically intimate?
2. What should the purpose of dating be? How should it be approached?
3. How can you personally prepare for marriage?

STOP SIGN
THE SABBATH

Simone Rizkallah

Remember the Sabbath day, to keep it holy. Six days you shall labor, and do all your work; but the seventh day is a sabbath to the Lord your God.

EXODUS 20:8–11

I have a confession to make. The first time I took my driver's-license test I did what natives in my land call the "California Roll." You've seen other drivers do it — it's when a driver doesn't brake properly when approaching a stop sign, but simply slows down and simply "rolls" through it. Needless to say, I failed my driver's test that day. But I learned an important lesson: Traffic laws exist for a reason. Taking the time to stop and check for oncoming traffic ensures safety on the road.

Similarly, the moral laws (otherwise known as the Ten Commandments) exist for a very good reason as well: our spiritual protection and ultimately our happiness. Let's take a look at my favorite commandment, the third one: to keep the Sabbath holy (cf. Ex 20:8). God himself told us to stop our busy lives and take time to replenish through worship and rest, especially when we feel "too busy." My driver's-license test was abruptly interrupted by the tester yelling "STOP" during my California Roll. Sometimes things happen that force us to stop and evaluate our lives in a meaningful way.

Stopping allows us to take a deep breath and refuel. We might be tempted to refuse to stop, believing that we are too busy. But without rest, life is just an endless cycle of pressure, school, work, motion, and eventually burnout. Time is always ticking, but we always manage to find time for what matters to us. Saint John Paul the Great encouraged us to dismiss apprehension. "Do not be afraid to give your time to Christ! Yes, let's open our time to Christ that he may cast light upon it and give it direction. He is the one who knows the secret of time and the secret of eternity, and he gives us 'his day' as an ever new gift of his love ... time given to Christ is never time lost, but is rather time gained, so that our relationships indeed our whole life may become more profoundly human."[89] In our busyness, we are often tempted to believe that everything relies on our actions. Indeed, "There is a risk ... (to) forget that God is the Creator upon which everything depends."[90] If we celebrate it rightly, Sunday offers us perspective on the road ahead, holy direction, and renewed strength in continuing each week's journey. In the words of Saint John Paul II, "Rest is something 'sacred,' because it is man's way of withdrawing from the sometimes excessively demanding cycle of earthly tasks in order to renew his awareness that everything is the work of God."[91] Let me invite you "to rediscover with new intensity the meaning of Sunday: its 'mystery', its celebration, its significance for Christians and human life."[92]

The Stop sign's eight-sided shape can be another

reminder to honor the third commandment. The Christian Sabbath is not only a day of rest from work, but also even more significantly a reminder of our eternal rest; namely, heaven. The "Lord's Day" (as Sunday was called from apostolic times), or Sunday, is known as the "eighth" day or the "day of the Resurrection" (CCC 1166). In order to understand how it is that Sunday is also the

PIT STOP

NATIONAL MUSEUM OF THE U.S. AIR FORCE
Riverside, Ohio

At the world's largest military aviation museum, and the official museum of the USAF, over 360 aircraft and missiles are on display, from the early days of flight to space shuttles.

"eighth" day, we have to fast-forward to the New Testament and to the newness that God's Son, Jesus Christ, brings to our lives. The *Catechism of the Catholic Church* explains: "The day of Christ's Resurrection is both the first day of the week, the memorial of the first day of creation, and the 'eighth day,' on which Christ after his 'rest' on the great sabbath inaugurates the 'day that the Lord has made,' the 'day that knows no evening'" (CCC 1166). The "eighth day" is when we Christians, here and now, still on this earth and in this life, begin to taste the "new heaven and the new earth" (Rv 21:1).

For Moses and the Israelites who received the Decalogue (the Ten Commandments), the third commandment is a day of rest for everyone and a remembrance of the world's creation. The Israelites, as well as modern-day Jews, traditionally celebrate the Sabbath day of rest from sunset on Friday to sunset on Saturday. I remember driving through certain Jewish neighborhoods when I lived in Los Angeles and seeing Orthodox Jews walking to synagogue to celebrate "Shabbat," which is "Sabbath" in Hebrew (it literally means "rest"). The Jewish observance of the Sabbath is a memorial of the liberation from the physical bondage of the Egyptians (cf. Ex 6:6) and the spiritual bondage to idols and the false gods of Egypt. Modern Orthodox Jews celebrate the third commandment so seriously that they do not even drive a car or use technology on the Sabbath.

For Christians, Christ gives new meaning to the Sabbath. We fulfill the Sabbath commandment by observing a Saturday evening to Sunday rest, instead of the Jewish Friday evening to Saturday, because the newness of life in Christ is brought about through the miracle of the Resurrection: "The Lord's day, the day of the Resurrection, the day of Christians, is our day. It is called the Lord's day because on it the Lord rose victorious to the Father. If pagans call it the 'day of the sun,' we willingly agree, for today the light of the world is raised, today is revealed the sun of justice with healing in his rays" (CCC 1166).[93]

Every Sunday we celebrate the resurrection of Jesus, the promised resurrection of our own bodies (cf. Phil 3:20), and the eternal life we hope to share with God and each other. In a way, it is Easter every Sunday! But we don't celebrate it just as something past (as in the case of the Israelites being liberated from Egyptian bondage) or something in the future (when we are in heaven one day); we actually participate in it here and now. Sunday is an invitation to rejoice in an encounter with the risen Lord. The most important way to celebrate this feast day is through our presence at the Holy Sacrifice of the Mass and receiving the Eucharist. As my former priest-boss used to say, the Mass is when "heaven and earth kiss!" And that, my friends, is *anything* but boring. Going to Mass isn't one more thing to check off on a busy schedule, or a waste of time. It is the best thing to do! Truly, "seek first his kingdom … and all these things shall be yours as well" (Mt 6:33–34).

Attending Mass on Sundays, then, is the primary way we stop our busy lives to keep this third commandment. It is so important for our spiritual health and happiness that the Church calls it an obligation: "The Sunday Eucharist is the foundation and confirmation of all Christian practice. For this reason the faithful are obliged to participate in the Eucharist on days of obligation, unless excused for a serious reason (for example, illness, the care of infants) or dispensed

ROADSIDE DISTRACTIONS

Word of Life Mural ("Touchdown Jesus")

South Bend, Indiana

Saints and scholars through the ages look toward Christ in this mural adorning the University of Notre Dame's library. It's visible from the football stadium, hence the nickname "Touchdown Jesus."

by their own pastor. Those who deliberately fail in this obligation commit a grave sin" (CCC 2181).

By the way, in case you are wondering what "days of obligation" are, they are those days you must stop and go to Mass and refrain from servile work (remember, God gave us commandments — not options or suggestions!). Sunday is of course included, but there are other special obligatory feast days. Mark your calendar now: January 1 (Solemnity of Mary, Mother of God), the Feast of the Ascension (forty days after Easter; check with your parish), August 15 (Feast of the Assumption of Mary), November 1 (All Saints' Day), December 8 (Feast of the Immaculate Conception), and December 25 (you got this one, right?). These days are important events in salvation history, so going to Mass is a way of showing gratitude and celebrating our new life in Christ. At the high school where I teach, we are given these days off to be able to go to Mass and do something celebratory. For me, this often involves cupcakes. You might not get the day off from school or work, but you can plan to make your local parish's evening Mass and maybe add a special treat to your day.

But words like "obligation" and "grave sin" (CCC 2181) seem less like a call to celebrate and more like the Church being super bossy and trying to ruin your weekend fun. If this is what you think, let me propose to you a different perspective, one that often gets overlooked despite its simplicity. Sometimes you hear the Mass called "the Holy Sacrifice of the Mass"; but have you ever stopped to think about what that means? "Holy" means something dedicated to God, so we become "holy" when we offer our lives back to him who first gave us life. Who could have created a better road map for our lives than the one who created us in the first place? A "sacrifice" is something that is surrendered or given up. God's son became man and sacrificed his very self for our sins so that we could ultimately share in his life. Saint Paul writes, "For our sake he made him to be sin who knew no sin, so that in him we might become the righteousness of God" (2 Cor 5:21).

Lastly, the word "Mass" comes from the Latin "to be sent." When we attend and participate in the Mass, we are setting aside time for Jesus, to receive his Body, Blood, Soul, and Divinity in the Eucharist so that, transformed with this new life, we can be sent out into the world to spread the Gospel or "good news" of this new life with him both now and forever. Life is not just a journey; it is also a destination. It is a journey with the Lord and to the Lord. To put it bluntly, no matter how ugly the church building, or boring the homily, or annoying the people, or off-pitch the choir, the Eucharist is the most profound way that God shows his love for us because it is truly a gift of himself. Therefore, we love God in return when we receive the gift of his real presence in the Eucharist and bring others into this love as well.

Some people would rather sleep in and snack on a toaster treat than go to Mass to receive the Eucharist, the bread of life. This is a lack of spiritual vision and a case of misdirected priorities. In the past, Christians were often threatened with death just for attending Mass (as they still are today in some countries). In A.D. 304, the emperor Diocletian forbade the Christians in Abitene (in present-day Tunisia) to possess the Scriptures, to worship, or to build churches, "on pain of death."[94] But they refused to obey these "severe orders," declaring "we cannot live without joining on Sunday to celebrate the Eucharist. We would lack the strength to face our daily problems and not to succumb."[95] These holy men and women were tortured and killed, and are now known as the Forty-nine Martyrs of Abitene. If people have been willing to die for the sake of worship, it must be something incredibly special — worth getting up on a Sunday morning for!

The second part of the practical application of the third commandment has to do with the necessity of rest; or more precisely, leisure. Basically, God's not being mean. He just doesn't want you to crash and burn. He's our dad. He's not some senile grandpa in the sky handing you keys to the Porsche without basic instructions on where to go and how to get there. If you're too tired to drive, no way are you going to be able to go anywhere. Thankfully, this doesn't mean we can't drive cars or use technology on Sundays like the Orthodox Jews. (Although fasting from those things would be a very powerful way to pray.) It means you need to make this day special by not doing *unnecessary* work. Once again, this is for our personal happiness and flourishing, as the *Catechism* clarifies: "Just as God 'rested on the seventh day from all his work which he had done,' human life has a rhythm of work and rest. The institution of the Lord's Day helps everyone enjoy adequate rest and leisure to cultivate their familial, cultural, social, and religious lives" (CCC 2184).

HOLY ROAD TRIP

BLESSED SOLANUS CASEY CENTER

Detroit, Michigan

Blessed Solanus served at this Capuchin monastery, which now holds his tomb and a museum in his memory. He helped many people with his prayers and intercession.

Here's some good news: God might not want you to be doing your homework or chores on the Sabbath. Does that mean God doesn't want you to do your homework or chores in general? You know the answer to this one. The beauty of the Sabbath is that it allows you to order your life in such a way that you are not rolling through it at full speed. Sabbaths aren't just for Sundays, but for all days of the week. In order to keep a proper Sabbath, you must prioritize your life in such a way that God is at the center — not because he needs it, but because you (and I) need it. It's pretty hard to make excuses on this one. Are you really going to tell the Creator, the one who literally made time, that you don't have time for him?

I am a high school teacher, and when some of my students show up on Monday morning, tempted to snooze through my class, I know they have not kept a proper Sabbath and that now they will be cranky, tired, and unhappy for most of the week. These students tend to roll through life without ever stopping to consider that they were made for more. Saint Irenaeus, an early Church Father, once said, "The glory of God is man fully alive!" Who can honestly say that type of life isn't appealing?

As Pope St. John Paul II wrote, "When Sunday loses its fundamental meaning and becomes merely part of a 'weekend,' it can happen that people stay locked within a horizon so limited that they can no longer see 'the heavens.'"[96] Skipping the Sabbath celebration can lead us to forget our story as Christians. The weekend is about rest and relaxation, but the Sabbath offers us something more. "The grace flowing from this wellspring [the Mass] renews mankind, life and history."[97]

This isn't just about resting or getting enough sleep, however, but about becoming who you were created to be. God didn't create us to be his slaves, his servants, or hired help. He doesn't need us at all. He is perfectly happy in and of himself. So why did God create us? He created us for our sake, our good, and our happiness. He created us to know and love him and ultimately to be friends with him. Jesus said to his disciples, "No longer do I call you servants ... but I have called you friends"

(Jn 15:15). This is what the Christian faith is primarily about: friendship with the Holy Trinity. Keeping the third commandment gives us the opportunity to develop that friendship.

Sunday is our day to "hang out" with God and with each other. It's also an excellent time to do those leisurely activities that one does for their own sake. Pope Francis says that "together with a culture of work, there must be a culture of leisure as gratification. To put it another way: people who work must take the time to relax, to be with their families, to enjoy themselves, read, listen to music, play a sport. But this is being destroyed, in large part, by the elimination of the Sabbath rest day."[98] When we engage in these leisurely activities, we are expressing the depth of our unique humanity, since we are made in God's "image and likeness" (Gn 1:27). Animals don't have an intellect and a will. They don't ponder the meaning of life, write books on philosophy, or take vacations.

Another aspect of Sunday with Jesus is serving others. On Sunday, consider visiting some older adults who are isolated, look to feed the homeless, or go out of your way to help your parents. The Mass and the Eucharist nourish us, and in receiving we are able to give of ourselves. Of course acts of service shouldn't be restricted to just Sunday, but it is a good place to start!

Besides going to Mass and avoiding unnecessary work, the way we choose to spend our Sabbath rest is up to our conscience. Perhaps you decided not to go shopping on Sundays, but your mother is sick and needs cold medicine. Is it okay for you to go to the pharmacy? Of course! Jesus teaches us not to miss the point of the commandment: "The sabbath was made for man, not man for the sabbath" (Mk 2:27).

What happens when you starting living a Sabbath paradigm of life? Well, try it out and see! Take a moment to reflect on your lifestyle right now. Do you celebrate a "secular Sabbath" on Friday night instead of a "holy Sabbath" on Sunday? Are you going to Mass on Sundays? Are you making enough quality time for your family and your friends? Do you pursue leisurely activities that bring you joy? Or are you burned out (like many of my students) from the stress of schoolwork, sports, and feeling like you are always playing catch-up?

God is merciful. He wants you to enjoy life and live the freedom you were destined for. Without proper worship and play, this will become impossible. It is important to intentionally build a Sabbath way of life. One of the ways that I make Sunday special is to have a Saturday night "Lord's Day dinner" with my friends. It's a ritual similar to the Jewish Shabbat dinner. We gather together, sing some songs on the guitar, eat dinner (sometimes we bring the traditional Jewish challah bread! Yum!), read the Gospel for that Sunday's Mass, and share our blessings from the previous week. It doesn't replace Mass, but it makes ending and beginning the week (living the "eighth" day) an occasion to intentionally relax with my best friends in another way. What can you do to make the Sabbath special?

Shabbat shalom! Good Lord's Day to you and yours!

QUESTIONS FOR REFLECTION

1. What takes number one priority in your life? Do you feel like you are too busy?
2. Why is attending and participating in the Mass so vital to your life? How can you enter into the Lord's Day better, and cultivate a spirit of celebration?
3. What is leisure? Does it have a place in your life? How can it be a source of rest and inspiration?

BLIND PEDESTRIAN
SPIRITUAL SIGHT

Jennessa Terraccino

Receive your sight; your faith has made you well.

LUKE 18:42

Perhaps on one of your driving adventures or casual drives through your neighborhood, you have caught sight of a Blind Pedestrian sign. This sign is posted to alert drivers that a blind person lives close by and travels the nearby streets. When encountering such a sign, you should slow down and keep your eyes open for someone walking with a seeing-eye dog or a white walking stick outstretched in front of them. A blind person won't see you, so you will have to watch out for them. As you drive by, you may wonder to yourself who the blind pedestrian is: a little girl, someone your own age, or maybe an older adult? What if you were the one who was blind? How would losing your sight affect you?

In truth, on the road of life, many souls have become blind pedestrians, but maybe not in the way you are thinking. Not surprisingly, the word blind is not a positive word. Its synonyms include visionless, dark, and even eyeless. Surely being physically blind is a cross to bear. Darkness fills pupils instead of light, color, and all the visual beauty life has to offer. In the same way, when spiritual vision is lacking, a spiritual darkness shadows the beauty of a life with Christ. According to Pope Benedict XVI, physical blindness "has great significance in the Gospels" because it "represents man who needs God's light, the light of faith, if he is to know reality truly and to walk the path of life."[99] Those who are blind pedestrians lack faith and vision for Christ and his holy Church. "Their eyes they have closed, lest they should perceive with their eyes ... and understand with their heart, and turn for me to heal them" (Mt 13:15). Truly, many people are not able to see that Jesus is indeed the very desire of their heart. Such individuals have allowed themselves to be blinded to the truth by the world.

If you were blind, would you want to be picked up and sat in your friend's backseat, and be driven around town? Such an act would be very kind of them, and very helpful to you. But when we take a backseat to the Faith, even if it's to a driver we trust, we're in trouble. If you've become a blind follower on the road of life, instead of the driver, you may fall prey to being "tossed back and forth and carried about with every wind of doctrine" (Eph 4:14). Do you let peers guide the way you will live and what you will believe?

A friend of mine once shared some key "new driver" advice that she had learned from her driver's ed teacher. Her teacher wanted to give students a heads-up; he said, "When you sneeze, your eyes will temporarily close. Remain calm, with your hands steady on the wheel." Sometimes we are surprised by a sneeze, and we lose sight of the road before us for a few seconds. It can be a bit alarming. On life's road, we may have moments of darkness: a tested faith, consuming doubts, or times when temptation turns to sin, and we take our eyes off the target, Christ.

As long as we drive through these "sneezes" or moments of darkness with prayer, confession, and spiritual counsel, the road ahead will eventually beam bright again. Therefore, a bigger concern is if you fall asleep at the wheel. That would be some seriously blind driv-

PIT STOP

ALCATRAZ ISLAND

San Francisco, California

Besides the abandoned prison, Alcatraz holds an old lighthouse, early military fortifications, art installations, natural features, and a myriad of bird species, making it a fascinating day trip.

ing. In the spiritual life, these are the folks who choose darkness over light: "The light has come into the world, and men loved darkness rather than light" (Jn 3:19). This is a dark journey without headlights or hope. It is a life rooted in sin, self, and dreamy distraction. That's a scary way to journey! For, "he who walks in the darkness does not know where he goes" (Jn 12:35). Without Christ, it is all pointless meandering.

Those dedicated to Christ are far from blind. "For you are all sons of light and sons of the day; we are not of the night or of the darkness. So then let us not sleep, as others do, but let us keep awake" (1 Thes 5:5–6). As Christ's children on the road, it is important that we never sleep at the wheel. Instead, drive with your heavenly headlights turned on, proclaiming: "You are my lamp, O Lord, and my God lightens my darkness" (2 Sm 22:29). A journey with light and toward the light makes for a purposeful pilgrimage toward heaven (see "Road

Narrows: Heaven"). Pope Francis reminds us that "God is the light that illuminates the darkness … and a spark of divine life is within each of us."[100] Do not let the light of Christ burn out in you!

Beware of spiritual blindness on the road of life! Such darkness, which leads to a lack of faith, can consume you in two primarily different ways. The first is by perpetuating a life of sin. When material goods and fleshly desires become a god, your soul's vision is altered. The Devil becomes a guide and god snatching the light out of you. "The god of this world has blinded the minds of the unbelievers, to keep them from seeing the light of the gospel of the glory of Christ" (2 Cor 4:4). A life rooted in sin will propel you away from those who are of the light, and keep you a blind pedestrian.

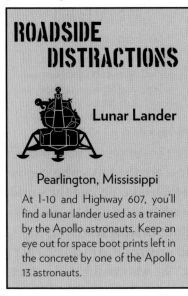

ROADSIDE DISTRACTIONS

Lunar Lander

Pearlington, Mississippi

At I-10 and Highway 607, you'll find a lunar lander used as a trainer by the Apollo astronauts. Keep an eye out for space boot prints left in the concrete by one of the Apollo 13 astronauts.

If someone is without the Savior, our Lord Jesus, he or she becomes his or her own god. In America, self-worship, the second cause of blindness, is one big pothole that's easy to fall into — thanks to social media, a "me" mentality, extreme emphasis on top-notch colleges and careers, an obsession with personal accomplishments, greed for cash, and seeking after a lifestyle of cars, mansions, and more. "For you say, I am rich, I have prospered, and I need nothing; not knowing that you are wretched, pitiable, poor, blind, and naked" (Rv 3:17).

Venerable Fulton Sheen warns, "If you do not worship God, you worship something, and nine times out of ten it will be yourself."[101] The more the crown is placed upon your ego, the less the heart will be inclined to see past the self to the true king, Christ Jesus. Pope Francis also cautions us that "the most dangerous idol is our own selves when we want to occupy the place of God."[102]

If you worship and feed your own ego, you risk becoming blinded by your own splendor. All human beings reflect light because they are made in the "image" and "likeness" of God (Gn 1:26), but they are not *the* light; Christ is. "Jesus spoke to them saying, 'I am the light of the world'" (Jn 8:12). All God's creatures have a luminous quality. One angel in particular was named for light: Lucifer. But he fell from heaven when he believed himself to be more beautiful and magnificent than God. He was blinded by his own glory. "How you are fallen from heaven, O Day Star, son of Dawn! … You said in your heart … 'I will set my throne on high … I will make myself like the Most High.' But you are brought down to Sheol, to the depths of the Pit" (Is 14:12–15). Any light Lucifer once possessed was snuffed out when he chose his ego over communion with God. He lost it all, becoming Satan, and seeks to torment souls into the same dark destiny through deception.

In order to flee from darkness, we must follow in the spirit of Saint John the Baptist, who declared, "He must increase, but I must decrease" (Jn 3:30). Saint John the Baptist was considered the last prophet to prepare the way for Christ. "He was not the light, but came to bear witness to the light" (Jn 1:8).[103]

Would you say that you have been roaming as if you were a blind pedestrian, or with the light ever before you illuminating your way? Do you need a vision test to hold you accountable? When getting your license for the first time, or when renewing it, the motor vehicle department requires you to take the classic eye exam, the one with all those E's, F's, P's, and Z's. If you don't pass, you won't be given a license, and it might be time to polish that pair of glasses. If you were given a spiritual-vision test, would you pass? Do you read Scripture's letters, God's word, or is it fuzzy to you?

Two close disciples of Christ lacked the vision to see the Savior when they traveled the road to Emmaus. "While they were talking and discussing together, Jesus himself drew near and went with them. But their eyes were kept from recognizing him" (Lk 24:15–16). On their journey, these men were discussing Christ's Passion, and their own doubts and disappointments. They no longer believed that Jesus was the Savior. Lacking spiritual vision, they of course did not know that Jesus had risen and was in their very midst (cf. Lk 24:17–27).

Indeed, Jesus is the Savior of the world, but they did not recognize him because of their blindness. How then did they come to see the truth? It was when Jesus remained with them and "took the bread and blessed, and broke it, and gave it to them. And their eyes were opened and they recognized him" (Lk 24:30–31). In other words, the Eucharistic Christ healed their spiritual blindness. This is the very way our blindness can be healed too. Even today the light of Christ can fill our blind hearts when we pray the Rosary, perhaps meditating on the Institution of the Eucharist in the Luminous Mysteries while praying before Jesus in the Blessed Sacrament, or when consuming his Body, Blood, Soul, and Divinity at Holy Mass. On the road, may we multiply our Eucharistic encounters, seeking to walk with Christ always with our eyes wide open to him.

If you struggle with blindness, continue to seek Christ. Renew your dedication to him. Jesus can heal us from anything (cf. Mt 21:14; Lk 7:21). Miracles are still possible today! Throughout the Gospels, Jesus healed countless individuals, including the blind. "Two blind men followed him, crying aloud, 'Have mercy on us, Son of David.' When he entered the house, the blind men came to him; and Jesus said to them, 'Do you believe that I am able to do this?' They said to him, 'Yes, Lord.' Then he touched their eyes, saying, 'According to your faith be it done to you.' And their eyes were opened" (Mt 9:27–30). Our depth of faith both saves and limits us. If you are lukewarm, don't expect to move mountains.

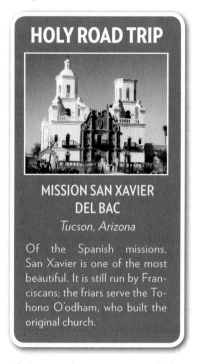

HOLY ROAD TRIP

MISSION SAN XAVIER DEL BAC

Tucson, Arizona

Of the Spanish missions, San Xavier is one of the most beautiful. It is still run by Franciscans; the friars serve the Tohono O'odham, who built the original church.

Do you trust that Christ can do great things in your life? Do you have the courage to call out to him? Do you desire to be healed?

It is okay to approach Jesus in your brokenness; in fact, it is key. Because Jesus is the Son of God, perfect beyond measure, it can be easy to feel we can come to him only if and when we are perfect. Yet that's completely backward. Jesus beckons the weak. He wants our brokenness. We need a messiah. We cannot save ourselves. Our ego, success, money, friends, boyfriend or girlfriend, possessions, or food choices cannot save us.

If the entire world ended tomorrow, none of that would matter! This is the very reason he came into the world: to save us from sin, and from all that makes us broken and blind. Perfection and salvation are impossible without Christ. He is our eternal light and treasure!

Seek out the light, and humble yourself at the feet of Christ. Ask him to continue to convert your heart, and to strengthen your faith and trust in him. Ask him to heal you from sinful inclinations, habitual sins, personal struggles and weaknesses, and even physical ailments. Ask him to give you a true spiritual vision and to remove any blindness, just as one man in Scripture did: "Lord, let me receive my sight" (Lk 18:41). Jesus is alive! He is real. He hears you, and can heal you if you but only approach him in prayer, in the Sacrament of Reconciliation, and through the Eucharist. To one blind man, and now to us, Jesus says: "Receive your sight; your faith has made you well" (Lk 18:42).

As children of the light, healed of our blindness, it is our job to shine the light of Christ to those around us. Be on the lookout for signs of blind pedestrians, or of blind peers in your car's backseat. In Scripture, those who were healed by Christ desired to proclaim it. Let us follow their example. It can be easy to shy away from sharing. Begin sharing the Gospel message by sharing what Christ has done in your own life: an answered prayer, a good life choice, and so forth. But start gently, careful not to come off too strong too soon. When encountering nonbelievers, pray for their spiritual healing, especially for a soft heart. Love Christ with all your heart so that you can be an authentic witness. Seek to answer any questions with love, knowledge, sincerity, and a peaceful manner. Also, be willing to invite others to meet Christ in your home, at your parish, or at events.

In the Gospels, there are many instances where, when the sick couldn't help themselves, others brought them to Christ. Bring the blind to Christ, who looks to heal them: "I will lead the blind in a way that they know not, in paths that they have not known I will guide them. I will turn the darkness before them into light" (Is 42:16).

As you journey, continue to resist any temptations toward becoming a blind pedestrian yourself. Keep your eyes fixed on the light of Christ, and your heart steadfast in faith. Stay on the road that is carrying you to the city of light: "And the city has no need of sun or moon to shine upon it, for the glory of God is its light, and its lamp is the Lamb" (Rv 21:23).

QUESTIONS FOR REFLECTION

1. What does physical blindness represent in the Gospel?
2. What are some ways spiritual blindness can consume you on the road of life? How can spiritual blindness be remedied?
3. Would you say that you have been roaming like a blind pedestrian, or with the light ever before you illuminating your way? In what ways?

FIRE ENGINE CROSSING
THE CALL AND NEED TO EVANGELIZE

Brian Pedraza

Whoever loses his life for my sake will find it.

MATTHEW 16:25

Growing up, I knew that our next-door neighbor was a nice man; that he always smiled and waved whenever he came home from work while my brother and I were playing basketball in the evening. I knew that he and his wife gave out the best Halloween candy. I knew that he had the best lawn in the neighborhood and I knew that he did some sort of work with the fire department.

But one day his wife came to our door, her face worn by tears, and gave me some of his old baseball caps. You see, her husband was a fire inspector, a man who checked out buildings to make sure they were safe, and who examined the remains of buildings after fire had consumed them to find out what started the fires so as to prevent such outbreaks from happening again. Many old buildings, it turns out, were made with the mineral asbestos, but it wasn't until the end of the twentieth century that we learned that breathing in particles of as-

169

bestos can cause cancer. In those charcoaled remains of buildings, my neighbor had breathed in huge amounts of asbestos. He literally gave his life to help others, and his wife wanted me to have some of his old baseball caps to remember him.

"Greater love has no man than this, that a man lay down his life for his friends" (Jn 15:13). This teaching of Jesus was something that the late Pope St. John Paul II reflected upon over and over again in his own teachings. The Pope recognized in Jesus' words the truth that we are made for love. Indeed, we can only truly find ourselves by giving of ourselves. This is what the pope called "the Law of the Gift," and it holds for us just as much as the law of gravity does. Drop this book and it falls to the ground. Even if you try to defy gravity by throwing the book in the air, you'll eventually lose as the book comes back down to the earth. The same goes for the Law of the Gift: it is inescapably true that, if you want to be the best version of yourself, you have to give of yourself to others.

I think that's why whenever I see a Fire Engine Crossing sign, I can't help but feel immense respect for the men and women, like my neighbor, who give of their lives to save others. They serve as a wonderful example that human beings are made to love, to give, to serve others. We admire people like them because, deep down, we know that their actions are a model of what it means to be a good human being. Even though I never fully appreciated what my neighbor did for a living, the baseball caps his wife gave me were an important reminder of the kind of man he was. They're an important reminder that the more we give of ourselves, the fuller we become. Or as Jesus put it, "Whoever loses his life for my sake will find it" (Mt 16:25).

Now, we won't all have the opportunity to literally give our lives for other people, but self-gift can take many forms. I work with college students, and recently one of them told me about the moment in which he felt the "fullest" in high school, the moment in which he was the best version of himself. Well-liked and respected by his

PIT STOP

NEWPORT MANSIONS
Newport, Rhode Island
These magnificent estates with their grand mansions are the American version of Europe's castles. Explore the homes, gardens, and summer "cottages" of a bygone era.

teammates, he was the starting safety on the football team. One game, he jumped in front of the offensive receiver and intercepted the ball. As he was running the interception back in hopes of scoring a touchdown, he noticed a junior on his team running behind him. Instead of scoring himself, he pitched the ball back to his teammate, who ran into the end zone for a touchdown. The crowd roared, and everyone cheered his teammate. Crazy, isn't it? My student felt like the fullest version of himself not when he decided to claim the glory all for himself, but when he chose to give it to someone else. It's exactly in moments like these when the Law of the Gift proves itself again.

What does this law mean for Christians — for us, who have experienced and been transformed by the love of Jesus Christ? Christians know that the greatest treasure, the most precious thing a human could experience, is the love of God. The love of God heals the sick, saves sinners, makes the weak strong, and turns beggars into children of God. "To fall in love with God," Saint Augustine said, "is the greatest of romances, to seek him the greatest adventure, to find him the greatest human achievement." The Law of the Gift plays an especially important role for Christians, then, when they share the love of God with others. Sharing this love is what the Church calls "evangelization," and it may just be the most important way a Christian is called to give of him- or herself to another person. But if you have to give of yourself to truly find yourself, as Jesus said, then we can put this truth even more boldly: it's impossible to be a Christian without sharing the Good News — that God has loved us in Jesus Christ — with other people. Saint Paul recognized this when he exclaimed, "Woe to me if I do not preach the Gospel!" (1 Cor 9:16).

ROADSIDE DISTRACTIONS

Enchanted Highway

Regent, North Dakota

Along this two-lane road, you'll find a collection of massive scrap metal sculptures, from pheasants to farmers. Each has parking and picnic areas, making this a scenic and comfortable detour.

So it is one of the rules of the Christian road that you must evangelize. If this is hard to take or sounds a little scary — don't worry. You're in good company. The Bible is filled with stories of people whom God asked to carry his word to others, and their responses show us they also found it hard at first. Moses, the greatest of the prophets, whom God chose to lead his people out of slavery and into the promised land? He thought the Israelites wouldn't believe him and that he wasn't a good enough speaker. Saint Peter, the first pope and the leader of the twelve Apostles? He threw himself at the feet of Jesus, ashamed at his own lack of belief. Actually, having a little humility like Moses and Peter is the perfect place to start when you realize that you are called to evangelize. Humility allows us to share the Good News with love and genuine care for others. A Catholic deacon I respect greatly once told me that the truth is not a possession we offer from our high-seated perch. Rather, "we're just beggars telling other people where we found the Bread." When we realize that we're all beggars before God, we can evangelize from a place of love rather than pride.

Realizing that we're all beggars also shows us that the message we must give others is truly "good" news. Even when it challenges us to change our lives, the Gospel is not meant to be an act of condemnation. It's the news of salvation. There's a big difference between sharing something with someone so that they will feel condemned and sharing it so that they will know they can be saved. The word "Gospel" itself is an English translation of a Greek word, *euangelion*, that was used by the ancient Greeks when a messenger would bring the "good news" of a victory in battle. Just as the messenger's words brought joy to the people, so should the Good News of Jesus' victory over sin and death bring joy to the people we evangelize.

But you can't lead anyone to the Bread if you've never found it or tasted it yourself. If you tell a friend who trusts you, "I've found some bread that will change your life," she's quite naturally going to want to know where you found it and what it tastes like. If you've never experienced Jesus, who is the Bread of Life (cf. Jn 6:35), you won't have a good answer. You've got to open yourself to receiving him before you can give him to others. As Pope Francis says:

> What kind of love would not feel the need to speak of the beloved, to point him out, to make him known? If we do not feel an intense desire to share this love, we need to pray insistently that he will once more touch our hearts. We need to implore his grace daily, asking him to open our cold hearts and shake up our luke-warm and superficial existence. ... How good it is to stand before a crucifix, or on our knees before the Blessed Sacrament, and simply to be in his presence! How much good it does us when he once more touches our lives and impels us to share his new life! ... There is nothing more precious which we can give to others.[104]

Talk to a priest you find inspiring, or to older brothers and sisters further ahead on the road to holiness whose faith you admire — and ask them how they came to know Jesus. Ask your friends who have faith how they've come to know him. Start reading the Bible, especially the Gospels, which tell about Jesus' life. Serve the poor, and see what they have to teach you about God. Pay closer attention to the words and actions of the Mass, and see if they have something new to tell you that you've never noticed before. Finally, pray, and be utterly honest before God, even if your prayer is, "Jesus, I want to know you but I don't even know how!" The more open and honest you are before God, and the more time you spend with him or even just seeking him, the more you will find that you are starting to really know him personally. When we genuinely seek God, we find him, because God is always seeking us first (CCC 2567).

Then, when you have finally tasted the Bread of Life and experienced the love of Jesus Christ in your own life, you will find that you can't help but want to share that love with others. If you've ever been in love before, you know that you just naturally want to talk about it with your friends and family. So it is for the person who has experienced the love of Christ. The desire to share that love just wells up inside. Love always seems to overflow so that it can draw other people in. "For if we have received the love which restores meaning to our lives, how can we fail to share that love with others?"[105]

All that being said, let's return to the Fire Engine Crossing sign. A Christian is a lot like a firefighter. He must be someone who gives of himself — sharing the saving gift of the Gospel — in order to save others from destruction. As long as we remember that we're fellow beggars and that our message is one of Good News, this is a great way to interpret that sign. We are called to save others from fire!

But there's another way to understand the significance of fire. For instance, sometimes we say that an athlete is "on fire." It's as if the person is so consumed in excellence that they are a marvel to behold. They capture our eyes the way a campfire holds everyone's gaze. Consider, too, all those movies set in medieval times, where blacksmiths forge and temper weapons by placing them in fire. So, fire is not always a cause of destruction, but when harnessed correctly, it has its good purposes, too.

I think it's this other way of understanding fire that Jesus had in mind when he said, "I came to cast fire upon the earth; and would that it were already kindled"

(Lk 12:49)! Just like a blacksmith, Jesus wants the "fire" of the Gospel to purify and strengthen the world. As followers of Christ, we are supposed to be so alive with the Gospel that we could be called "on fire." An amazing woman of God and doctor of the Church, Saint Catherine of Siena, said, "If you are who you should be you will set the world on fire."

If you are who you should be … how will you become whom God made you to be? Like the first Apostles, you will need boldness, perseverance, humility, and prayer. Spend time with the book of Acts, where you will read how Jesus' first followers often prayed for boldness even in the face of suffering (cf. Acts 4:29–31). Yes, being a Christian takes courage. But there are lots of great examples to inspire us.

Take, for instance, some of the students I worked with at Cornell University. They were part of a community they called "Souldiers," because they wanted to be people who evangelized their fellow college students with courage. One night, two of the Souldiers, Tim and Mike, were walking the streets of Collegetown just as the bars were letting out. Mike had his guitar, so he started strumming away. They improvised lyrics, joked, laughed, and greeted the students walking by, some of whom would say, "Did that guy just say hello to me?"

At one point, two guys came across the street and asked how long Tim and Mike had been playing music. Mike said "fifteen years," and Tim said with a smile, "I don't really do music." Somewhere along in the conversation Tim asked what they were up to tonight, and one guy answered that they were just looking "to get [high]." Tim, feeling the promptings of the Spirit, followed with, "I got what you need," and they asked what he had. He told them that they probably couldn't handle it, and began to back away from them. You could see their excitement and anxiousness growing by the second.

Then he said, "I don't think you guys are ready for this stuff, though. I'm gonna go find someone else." They could barely take it. They wouldn't let Tim take a step anywhere.

"Come on man, whatever you got, I want it!" they said.

"You really want to know what I got?"

"Heck yeah!"

"I've got the love of God and the joy that comes from the fulfillment of a life lived in Jesus Christ, and brother, this is your wake-up call."

Tim says he's never seen a smile change so quickly to a look of confusion and astonishment. "Dang, man, that's real," said one of the guys. Then Tim began to sincerely open up larger parts of his heart, speaking the truth of the Good News to them. They were touched. As they were about to leave, Tim asked, "Hey, can I pray with you guys quick before you take off?" They both agreed without hesitation, and soon there was a circle of men with their arms around each other in the middle of Collegetown.

After praying from the heart and asking the Lord to grant these men to labor beside him, Tim looked up and saw tears in one guy's eyes. The guy looked at his buddy and said, "This is no joke," and his buddy said, "Yeah man, I know."

A lot can happen when we let God inspire us to be Spirit-led evangelizers in the world.

Tim's style may not be your style, and what he said to those men may not have worked with other people. But when we take the time to reflect upon our personal gifts and to listen to the promptings of the Holy Spirit, allowing him to set us on fire, we grow in our ability to spread the Good News. Amazing conversations can happen in the streets of Collegetown, but they can also happen over a cup of coffee, at a sporting event, or at the lunch table. But whatever the situation, we are called to speak the truth, and to speak the truth with love. I admit it's not always an easy balance, but we need both. The Christian who knows the truth but lacks love may be right, but no one will listen to him if he's a jerk. The Christian who loves other people but doesn't ground that love in the truth will find that she is unable to change others' lives.

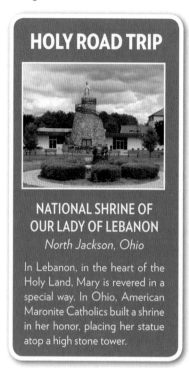

HOLY ROAD TRIP

NATIONAL SHRINE OF OUR LADY OF LEBANON
North Jackson, Ohio

In Lebanon, in the heart of the Holy Land, Mary is revered in a special way. In Ohio, American Maronite Catholics built a shrine in her honor, placing her statue atop a high stone tower.

So take a look around. Think of the people on the road of life with you, those you encounter day in and day out. How and where do they need to be loved? How can you start loving them so that a friendship builds to the point where you can offer the best gift of love to them, the gift of the Gospel? As you take to the roads, remember that God created you to love other people, to give completely of yourself so that they might have the fullness of life. We are beggars, but we have found the most precious gift, one so precious that we are set on fire, compelled to tell others where we found it (cf. 2 Cor 5:14). "It is the love of Christ that fills our hearts and impels us to evangelize. Today as in the past, he sends us through the highways of the world to proclaim his Gospel to all the peoples of the earth."[106]

QUESTIONS FOR REFLECTION

1. What is "the Law of the Gift"? In what ways can we live this kind of love?

2. Do you find the call to sharing the Gospel intimidating? Why or why not? What virtues might be helpful in your mission to evangelize?

3. In your everyday life, how can you bring the Gospel to others?

4. How is a Christian like a firefighter? Considering another meaning of fire, how can you follow Saint Catherine of Siena's commission to "set the world on fire"?

CONCLUSION

Jennessa Terraccino

These shall be the exits of the city.

EZEKIEL 48:30

As you exit this book, our road trip is coming to an end, but the adventure is just beginning! Pope Francis says that "life is a journey, along different roads, different paths, which leave their mark on us."[107] Life, if you choose to take ownership of it, is not meaningless meandering; it is a purposeful pilgrimage with the Holy Spirit in the passenger seat. God has prepared a unique itinerary for each of his pilgrims. Every road you travel, every road sign you see has the potential to draw you closer to the path he has laid out for you to travel to him.

One thing is for sure: God doesn't want us traveling alone. Pope Francis reminds us, "We know in faith that Jesus seeks us out."[108] Jesus can speak through anything, even road signs. Each and every day, he is looking to love you, heal you, and mold you. Keep driving with him and toward him! He desires your friendship.

A few years ago, I traveled to Spain to walk the pilgrimage of the Camino de Santiago, or the Way of St. James. Along the road, I met many people from all different backgrounds who were all in search of direction and purpose; whether they knew it or not, they were all in search of Christ. Each day, each pilgrim knew exactly what he was to do that day: push ahead to the final destination, the Cathedral of St. James. During that pilgrimage, each of us had a purpose, simple as it was. But upon completing the walk, some pilgrims seemed to feel a sense of loss rather than gain. In an instant, they had lost their purpose. These sojourners failed to see the journey was not about them, but about Jesus. Jesus is the Way, and our way is toward him. The conclusion of any earthly pilgrimage is really just the beginning of a life with Christ. He is our answer, our purpose. He is the road. He is the finish line!

As you continue your life with Christ, keep the right kind of vision! Scripture directs you to "set your minds on things that are above, not on things that are on earth" (Col 3:1–3). Remember two things regarding road signs:

1. What if each road sign had a different meaning to each driver on the road? I think the answer is pretty obvious. The roadway would be complete chaos! Our faith gives us the right direction to follow, and guides us in this world toward eternity. Don't be swayed by false truths. Read the Gospels, pray, praise Christ, and frequent the sacraments to fuel up for the journey.

2. Keep driving with eyes of faith. God has more to say to you, more to do in your life, and he wants you home in heaven with him one day. You have many hours on the road ahead of you — don't waste them! Allow Jesus to continue to speak to you through all the ways he can reach

you in your life, even through road signs as you drive.

Saint Frances of Rome, patron saint of automobile drivers, pray for us.

Saint Christopher, patron saint of travelers and drivers, pray for us.

Our Lady of the Highway, pray for us.

NOTES

1. Diane Williams, "The Arbitron National In-Car Study, 2009 Edition," Arbitron Inc., accessed May 7, 2018, http://www.arbitron.com/downloads/InCarStudy2009.pdf.

2. Alphonsus Liguori, *Preparation for Death: Or, Considerations on the Eternal Truths*, ed. Eugene Grimm (Brooklyn: Redemptorist Fathers, 1926), 56.

3. Charles Pope, "The Night Prayer of the Church as a 'Rehearsal for Death,'" Community in Mission (blog), March 5, 2015, accessed May 9, 2018, http://blog.adw.org/2015/03/the-night-prayer-of-the-church-as-a-rehearsal-for-death/.

4. Charles J. Chaput, Render Unto Caesar: Serving the Nation by Living Our Catholic Beliefs in Political Life (New York: Image, 2012), 45.

5. Ibid.

6. Ibid.

7. Joseph Ratzinger, "Mass Pro Eligendo Romano Pontifice: Homily of His Eminence Card. Joseph Ratzinger," April 18, 2005, accessed May 8, 2018, http://www.vatican.va/gpII/documents/homily-pro-eligendo-pontifice_20050418_en.html.

8. Ibid.

9. Ibid.

10. Dorothy Day, *On Pilgrimage* (Grand Rapids, MI: Eerdmans, 1999), 84.

11. Benedict XVI, "To the German Pilgrims Gathered in Rome for the Inauguration Ceremony of the Pontificate," April 25, 2005, accessed May 12, 2018, http://w2.vatican.va/content/benedict-xvi/en/speeches/2005/april/documents/hf_ben-xvi_spe_20050425_german-pilgrims.html.

12. John Bosco, *Forty Dreams of St. John Bosco: From St. John Bosco's Biographical Memoirs* (Charlotte, NC: TAN Books, 2009).

13. "What Is a Sacramental?," *Baltimore Catechism #3*,

accessed May 12, 2018, http://www.baltimore-catechism.com/lesson27.htm, 1052.

14. Francis (Pope), *Evangelii Gaudium* (The Joy of the Gospel), November 24, 2013, accessed May 12, 2018, https://w2.vatican.va/content/francesco/en/apost_exhortations/documents/papa-francesco_esortazione-ap_20131124_evangelii-gaudium.html, 3.

15. Benedict XVI, *Spe Salvi* (Saved in Hope), November 30, 2007, accessed May 13, 2018, http://w2.vatican.va/content/benedict-xvi/en/encyclicals/documents/hf_ben-xvi_enc_20071130_spe-salvi.html, 46.

16. Maria Faustina Kowalska, *Diary: Divine Mercy in My Soul* (Stockbridge, MA: Marian Press, 2007), 20.

17. F. X. Schouppe, *Purgatory: Explained by the Lives and Legends of the Saints* (Charlotte, NC: TAN Books, 2012), 35–36.

18. Josemaría Escrivá, *The Forge* (Princeton, NJ: Scepter, 1988), 1041.

19. *Today's Missal Music Issue 2018* (Portland, OR: Oregon Catholic Press, 2017), #477.

20. C. S. Lewis, *The Great Divorce* (London: Collins, 2012), viii.

21. Ibid.

22. John Chrysostom, "The Paschal Sermon of St. John Chrysostom," accessed May 20, 2018, http://www.beliefnet.com/faiths/christianity/2000/05/the-paschal-sermon-of-st-john-chrysostom.aspx.

23. Francis (Pope), Twitter post, May 24, 2013, 3:00 a.m., https://twitter.com/Pontifex/status/337870587676487680.

24. Amy Welborn, *Prove it! Prayer* (Huntington, IN: Our Sunday Visitor, 2002), 55-56.

25. Ibid., 56.

26. Ibid., 48.

27. Ibid., 44.

28. Padre Pio, "Spiritual Maxims," in *The Quotable Saint:*

Words of Wisdom from Thomas Aquinas to Vincent De Paul, ed. Rosemary Ellen Guiley (New York: Facts on File, 2002), 131.

29. Francis (Pope), *Amoris Laetitia* (The Joy of Love), March 19, 2016, accessed May 14, 2018, https://w2.vatican.va/content/francesco/en/apost_exhortations/documents/papa-francesco_esortazione-ap_20160319_amoris-laetitia.html, 39.

30. Francis (Pope), *The Church of Mercy* (Chicago: Loyola Press, 2014), 138.

31. "Generation M2: Media in the Lives of 8- to 18-Year-Olds," The Henry J. Kaiser Family Foundation website, January 20, 2010, accessed May 15, 2018, https://www.kff.org/other/event/generation-m2-media-in-the-lives-of/.

32. Francis (Pope), *Gaudete et Exsultate* (Rejoice and Be Glad), March 19, 2018, accessed May 15, 2018, http://w2.vatican.va/content/francesco/en/apost_exhortations/documents/papa-francesco_esortazione-ap_20180319_gaudete-et-exsultate.html, 11.

33. John Paul II, *Fides et Ratio* (Faith and Reason), September 14, 1998, accessed May 29, 2018, http://w2.vatican.va/content/john-paul-ii/en/encyclicals/documents/hf_jp-ii_enc_14091998_fides-et-ratio.html, 1.

34. Ibid., 36

35. Ibid., 29.

36. Thomas E. Woods, *How the Catholic Church Built Western Civilization* (Washington, D.C.: Regnery, 2012), 68.

37. Ibid., 70.

38. Ibid., 95.

39. Ibid., 98.

40. Ibid., 100.

41. Ibid., 102.

42. John Paul II, *Fides et Ratio,* 43.

43. Paul J. Glenn, *A Tour of the Summa* (London: Catholic Way Publishing, 2015), 5.

44. Ibid.

45. Ibid.

46. Ibid.

47. Ibid.

48. Ibid.

49. Woods, *How the Catholic Church Built Western Civilization*, 79.

50. Congregation for the Doctrine of the Faith, "Norms Regarding the Manner of Proceeding in the Discernment of Presumed Apparitions or Revelations," February 25, 1978, accessed May 30, 2018, http://www.ewtn.com/library/CURIA/cdfappsrevs.HTM.

51. Ibid.

52. William Saunders, "Saint Juan Diego and Our Lady," Catholic Education Resource Center, accessed May 29, 2018, https://www.catholiceducation.org/en/culture/catholic-contributions/saint-juan-diego-and-our-lady.html.

53. "The Image of Our Lady of Guadalupe Poses Such a Threat to Atheists That They Will Go to Extraordinary Lengths to Discredit It," Abyssus Abbyssum Invocat/Deep Calls to Deep, August 25, 2013, accessed May 30, 2018, https://abyssum.org/2013/08/25/the-image-of-our-lady-of-guadalupe-poses-such-a-threat-to-atheists-that-they-will-go-to-extraordinary-lengths-to-discredit-it/.

54. Ibid.

55. Ibid.

56. Joan Carroll Cruz, *Eucharistic Miracles and Eucharistic Phenomena in the Lives of the Saints* (Charlotte, NC: TAN Books, 2010), 3.

57. Ibid., 6.

58. Ibid.

59. Patti Armstrong, "Eucharistic Miracle? 'Bleeding Host' Phenomenon Reported in Dioceses Worldwide," *National Catholic Register*, December 11, 2015, accessed May 30, 2018, http://www.ncregister.com/daily-news/eucharistic-miracle-bleeding-host-phenomenon-reported-in-dioceses-worldwide.

60. Ibid.

61. Ibid.

62. *Today's Missal Music Issue 2018*, #537.

63. John Paul II, "Man and Woman: A Mutual Gift for Each Other," February 6, 1980, accessed May 22, 2018, http://www.ewtn.com/library/papaldoc/jp2tb16.htm.

64. John Paul II, *Mulieris Dignitatem* (On the Dignity and Vocation of Women), August 15, 1988, accessed May 22, 2018, https://w2.vatican.va/content/john-paul-ii/en/apost_letters/1988/documents/hf_jp-ii_apl_19880815_mulieris-dignitatem.html#_edn39.

65. Markus MacGill, "What is the Link between Love and Oxytocin?," *MedicalNewsToday*, September 4, 2017, accessed May 22, 2018, https://www.medicalnewstoday.com/articles/275795.php.

66. Louann Brizendine, "Excerpt: 'The Male Brain,'" National Public Radio, July 13, 2010, accessed May 26, 2018, https://www.npr.org/templates/story/story.php?storyId=127401741.

67. A de Boer, E. M. Van Buel, and G. J. Ter Horst, "Love Is More than Just a Kiss: A Neurobiological Perspective on Love and Affection," *Neuroscience* 201 (2012): 114–24, doi:10.1016/j.neuroscience.2011.11.017.

68. Ibid.

69. Navneet Magon and Sanjay Kalra, "The Orgasmic History of Oxytocin: Love, Lust, and Labor," *Indian Journal of Endocrinology and Metabolism* 15, no. 7 (2011), doi:10.4103/2230-8210.84851.

70. MacGill, "What Is the Link between Love and Oxytocin?"

71. Louann Brizendine, *The Female Brain* (London: Bantam, 2006), 68.

72. Andrea Salonia, Rossella E. Nappi, Marina Pontillo, Rita Daverio, Antonella Smeraldi, Alberto Briganti, Fabio Fabbri, Giuseppe Zanni, Patrizio Rigatti, and Francesco Montorsi, "Menstrual Cycle–related Changes in Plasma Oxytocin Are Relevant to Normal Sexual Function in Healthy Women," *Hormones and Behavior* 47, no. 2 (2005): 164–69, doi:10.1016/j.yhbeh.2004.10.002.

73. Brizendine, *The Female Brain*, 68.

74. Joe S. McIlhaney and Freda McKissic Bush, *Hooked: New*

Science on How Casual Sex Is Affecting Our Children (Chicago: Northfield Publishing, 2008), 37.

75. Kerstin Uvnäs-Moberg, Linda Handlin, and Maria Petersson. "Self-soothing Behaviors with Particular Reference to Oxytocin Release Induced by Non-noxious Sensory Stimulation," *Frontiers in Psychology* 5 (2014), doi:10.3389/fpsyg.2014.01529.

76. A. de Boer et al., "Love Is More than Just a Kiss."

77. Jean Mercer, "Adolescence Is an Emotionally Dangerous Time When Teenagers Are Likely to Attempt or Commit Suicide," in *Child Development: Myths and Misunderstandings* (Thousand Oaks, CA: SAGE Publishing), 306–10, accessed June 29, 2012, doi:10.4135/9781452275529.n57.

78. A. de Boer et al., "Love is more than just a kiss."

79. Brizendine, *The Female Brain*, 75.

80. A. de Boer et al., "Love is more than just a kiss."

81. McIlhaney and Bush, *Hooked,* 79.

82. Mercer, "Adolescence Is an Emotionally Dangerous Time."

83. McIlhaney and Bush, *Hooked*, 32.

84. "Condom," Chastity Project, accessed April 16, 2018, https://chastityproject.com/qa/condom/.

85. "STD Risk and Oral Sex – CDC Fact Sheet," Centers for Disease Control and Prevention, January 4, 2017, accessed March 17, 2018, https://www.cdc.gov/std/healthcomm/stdfact-stdriskandoral-sex.htm.

86. "Won't Safe Sex Protect You from Getting an STD?," Chastity Project, accessed April 16, 2018, https://chastityproject.com/qa/wont-safe-sex-protect-you-from-getting-an-std/.

87. "Human Papillomavirus (HPV)," Centers for Disease Control and Prevention, December 20, 2016, accessed April 16, 2018, https://www.cdc.gov/hpv/parents/whatishpv.html.

88. Henry Bodkin, "Half of Abortions Due to Failed Contraception – New Report," The Telegraph, July 7, 2017, accessed March 17, 2018, https://www.telegraph.co.uk/news/2017/07/06/half-abortions-due-failed-contraception-new-report/.

89. John Paul II, *Dies Domini* (On Keeping the Lord's Day Holy), May 31, 1998, accessed May 17, 2018, w2.vatican.va/content/john-paul-ii/en/apost_letters/1998/documents/hf_jp-ii_apl_05071998_dies-domini.html, 7.

90. Ibid., 65.

91. Ibid., 65.

92. Ibid., 3.

93. Here's a fun piece of trivia: Americans generally get both Saturday and Sunday off because America was founded on Judeo-Christian beliefs and values. Religious freedom and expression have been part of America's values since her founding. Also, the seven-day workweek has a religious origin as opposed to a natural reason (unlike the month, which observes lunar cycles).

94. Benedict XVI, "Pastoral Visit to Bari for the Conclusion of the 24th National Eucharistic Congress," May 29, 2005, accessed May 17, 2018, http://w2.vatican.va/content/benedict-xvi/en/homilies/2005/documents/hf_ben-xvi_hom_20050529_bari.html.

95. Ibid.

96. John Paul II, *Dies Domini*, 4.

97. Ibid., 81.

98. Francis (Pope), Francesca Ambrogetti, and Sergio Rubin, *Pope Francis: Conversations with Jorge Bergoglio* (New York: New American Library, 2014), 19–20.

99. Benedict XVI, "Holy Mass for the Closing of the Synod of Bishops," October 28, 2012, accessed May 20, 2018, http://w2.vatican.va/content/benedict-xvi/en/homilies/2012/documents/hf_ben-xvi_hom_20121028_conclusione-sinodo.html.

100. Thomas C. Fox, "Francis: Papal Court Is 'Leprosy of Papacy,'" National Catholic Reporter, October 1, 2013, accessed May 20, 2018, https://www.ncronline.org/blogs/francis-chronicles/francis-papal-court-leprosy-papacy.

101. Fulton J. Sheen, *Remade for Happiness* (San Francisco: Ignatius Press, 2014), 14.

102. Francis (Pope) , *Pope Francis in His Own Words*, ed. Julie

Schwietert Collazo and Lisa Rogak (Novato, CA: New World Library, 2013), 46.

103. Interestingly, the Church celebrates St. John the Baptist's feast of nativity on June 24 every year. In the Northern Hemisphere, the longest day of the year, or summer solstice, is June 21. From that day on, each day becomes shorter until the winter solstice, which occurs anywhere from December 20 to the 23rd. The Church, of course, celebrates Jesus' nativity on December 25. It is upon the birth of Christ, the light of the world, that the days begin to lengthen again; whereas, the sunlight decreases after St. John the Baptist's birth. May this natural phenomenon remind you always to let Christ's light shine brighter than your own by giving Jesus first place in your life.

104. Francis (Pope), *Evangelii Gaudium*, 264.

105. Ibid., 8.

106. Benedict XVI, "Apostolic Letter Issued 'Motu Proprio' Porta Fidei for the Indiction of the Year of Faith," October 11, 2011, accessed May 17, 2018, http://w2.vatican.va/content/benedict-xvi/en/motu_proprio/documents/hf_ben-xvi_motu-proprio_20111011_porta-fidei.html, 7.

107. Francis (Pope), "Apostolic Journey of His Holiness Pope Francis to Cuba, to the United States of America, and Visit to the United Nations Headquarters," September 27, 2015, accessed May 29, 2018, https://w2.vatican.va/content/francesco/en/speeches/2015/september/documents/papa-francesco_20150927_usa-detenuti.html.

108. Ibid.

CONTRIBUTORS

Chelsea Zimmerman is the editor-in-chief of *CatholicLane. com*, and managing editor for *Ignitum Today* and *Catholic Stand*. In 1999, when she was a junior in high school, she suffered a spinal cord injury in a car accident that left her paralyzed from the chest down. Zimmerman was born and raised Catholic, and constantly strives to deepen her faith and strengthen her relationship with Christ and the Church. She has a strong devotion to the Immaculate Heart of Mary and the Rosary, and enjoys spiritual reading, spending time in front of the Blessed Sacrament, frequent confession, and going to daily Mass.

Mattias Caro teaches history classes for the Well-Trained Mind Academy; is Director of Curriculum for Good Shepherd School in Purcellville, Virginia; contributes as the executive editor of *Ethika Politika*, and remains a practicing attorney. He holds a BA in history from the College of William and Mary, a master's in theology from Christendom College Graduate School, and a JD from George Mason University. Mattias, his wife Katheryn, and their three children, seven chickens, and cat live in Hamilton, Virginia.

Jonna Schuster and her husband, Jim, have a heart for ecumenism and bringing encouragement and revitalization to the Catholic Church. They can be found at *www. catholicrevivalministries.com*. Joanna is a graduate of the University of Illinois and the Christendom College Graduate School, with degrees in graphic design and moral theology, respectively. She spent ten years as a full-time director of youth ministry in the Diocese of Arlington,

Virginia, before which she served for two years as a campus minister at Western Illinois University.

Ben Fleser has worked and volunteered in several youth and campus ministries in the Dioceses of Arlington and Richmond, Virginia. He graduated from George Mason University in 2010 with a degree in English and a minor in Film Studies, but his involvement with the Catholic Campus Ministry at GMU inspired him to pursue youth ministry upon graduation. His family is originally from Michigan, so he is an avid Detroit sports fan and has a strong devotion to Blessed Solanus Casey, who is buried in Detroit. In his free time, he still likes to skateboard, although it is becoming slightly more difficult at age thirty.

Emily Borman is the editor of *Conversation with Women*, a website for Catholic women. She is also a master catechist for the Diocese of Arlington, Virginia, and holds an Advanced Certificate in Youth Ministry from the Diocese of Arlington in conjunction with the Franciscan University of Steubenville. She is a freelance writer and editor, and also spends forty hours a week writing and editing for a government contractor. She and her husband Bill have been married for many years and are nearing an empty nest.

Miriam Marston serves as the coordinator for the Institute for Catholic Life and Leadership for the Archdiocese of Portland, Oregon. She has released two albums of original music, and two books as well. She received her BA in History and Religion from the College of William and Mary, and an MA in Pastoral Ministry from Boston College. Originally from Alexandria, Virginia, she moved to Oregon after eight years in Boston, where she worked for the Archdiocese of Boston in the office of canonical affairs, eventually moving into the role of Assistant Director of Lay Theology Programs at the Theological Institute at St. John's Seminary. Prior to Boston, she lived in Oxford, England, where she worked for a law firm and then a travel agency. One of her greatest joys is being an aunt to her beautiful nieces and nephews. Visit *www.miriammarston.com* to learn more.

Kimberly Cook is the author of *My Hand in Yours, Our Hands in His* and *Mommy, Mommy, When You Pray*, and the coauthor of *Once I Was Blind, But Now I See*. Her work regularly appears on Catholic news and journalism sites. Kimberly holds an MA in Systematic Theology and a BS in Mental Health, and runs *TheLionOfDesign.com*, an outlet for thought and discussion on faith and motherhood. She has worked for many years in ministry, and lives with her husband and four children in Virginia.

Allison Gingras is the founder of *ReconciledToYou.com*, where she shares the beauty of the Catholic Faith with honesty, laughter, and relatable examples from everyday life. She developed the *Stay Connected Journals for Catholic Women*, which include her book, *The Gift of Invitation: 7 Ways Jesus Invites You to a Life of Grace*. Allison hosts *A Seeking Heart with Allison Gingras*, a podcast on *BreadboxMedia.com*. She has written for *CatholicMom.com*, *Shalom Tidings*, *Catholic Stand*, *Catechist Magazine*, and more. Allison is a social media specialist for the

Kennedy Brownrigg Group and WINE: Women in the New Evangelization.

———

Carmen Briceño was consecrated into the Order of Virgins in 2009. She is the founder of Happy Feet Ministries, which allows her to evangelize youth, young adults, and families both in English and Spanish. To learn more about her speaking ministry, visit *www.happyfeetministries.com*. She also founded Sacred Print, which seeks to evangelize through art and beauty. All the products are geared to help people be bold in their faith by sharing sacred images of the lives of Jesus and the saints in their own community. A portion of the proceeds of Sacred Print go to Matthew 25, which is the homeless outreach she cofounded in 2016. Find out more at *www.etsy.com/shop/sacredprint*.

———

Keeley Bowler is an instructor of an intensive Theology of the Body course for teenagers, and has spent over eight years as a speaker helping teens to distinguish true love from convincing counterfeits. She also works as an independent consultant, providing market research and strategy advice to companies introducing disruptive technologies, especially in the life sciences. She helped grow a nonprofit organization focused on forming young adults and youths in the virtue of chastity and respect for the sanctity of life, Pure in Heart America (see *www.pureinheartamerica.org* for more information). She has a master's degree in Biochemistry from Brown University and a certificate in Bioethics from the National Catholic Center for Bioethics. Keeley is a proud wife and mother of three kids.

———

Simone Rizkallah is currently the senior theology teacher and a department chair at St. Mary's Catholic High School in Phoenix, Arizona. She has a graduate degree in Theological Studies with an emphasis on Systematic Theology from Christendom College. She worked professionally in marketing communications, media, radio, and theater before discovering her passion for the Faith and her call to teach and evangelize. As the daughter of immigrants from the Armenian diaspora in Cairo, Egypt, she has a particular interest in matters of religious freedom and culture. She helps lead the local chapters of the ecclesial movement Communion and Liberation and the Washington, D.C.–based nonprofit In Defense of Christians.

Brian Pedraza is currently a professor at Franciscan Missionaries of Our Lady University. He holds a PhD in Catechetics and Religious Education from the Catholic University of America. A blessed husband and a proud father, he was a high school teacher at De Sales High School in Geneva, New York, and served as the director of Souldiers Ministry at Cornell University and as the director of Catholic Outreach at Keuka College. His life is dedicated to the New Evangelization, and to forming others to be its heralds in the world.

ABOUT THE EDITOR

Jennessa Terraccino is the author of *The Princess Guide: Faith Lessons from Snow White, Cinderella & Sleeping Beauty* (Servant Books). She has earned an MA in Theological Studies and an Advanced Apostolic Catechetical Diploma from the Christendom College Graduate School. She also holds a certificate in youth ministry accredited by Franciscan University of Steubenville. Jennessa spent several years actively serving teens through her service as a volunteer and full-time youth director in the Diocese of Arlington, Virginia. She is passionate about serving teens and young adults, and seeks to enrich their lives through her speaking and writing apostolate. Jennessa currently resides in New England with her husband and children. You can connect with her online at *www.femmeorfaux.com*.